THE DARK HORSE:
THE MAKING OF A LITTLE MAG

ALSO BY GERRY CAMBRIDGE:

The Printed Snow: On Typesetting Poetry,
Happen*Stance* Press, 2015
Notes for Lighting a Fire,
Happen*Stance* Press, 2012, 2nd edition 2013
Aves (Prose Poems on Wild Birds), Essence Press, 2007
Madame Fi Fi's Farewell and Other Poems,
Luath Press, 2003
The Praise of Swans, Shoestring Press, 2000
*'Nothing But Heather!': Scottish Nature in Poems,
Photographs and Prose*, Luath Press, 1999; 2nd edition 2008
The Shell House, Scottish Cultural Press, 1995
The Dark Gift and Other Poems, St Inans Press, 1994

The Dark Horse:

The Making
of a Little Magazine

&

*Sundry Divagations
on Poets, Poetry,
Criticism*

&

Poetry Culture

GERRY CAMBRIDGE

Happen*Stance* Press

ISBN 978-1-910131-29-9

Typesetting and design by Gerry Cambridge
www.gerrycambridge.com

The author acknowledges the support of
Creative Scotland in the publication of
this volume.

Published in 2016 by Happen*Stance*
21 Hatton Green, Glenrothes, Fife KY7 4SD
nell@happenstancepress.com
www.happenstancepress.com

Printed and bound by Imprint Digital, Exeter
www.imprint.co.uk

For Dana Gioia

Acknowledgements & Thanks

Writing an account such as this one is a strange business. You think: who will be offended if I leave them out? Or, perhaps worse: who will be offended, indeed, if I include them? For any such omissions or inclusions, my apologies in advance.

This is my memory of *The Dark Horse*'s place in the literary scene at a particular period. Written at another point, it would have been different—certainly in some of its incidentals and, doubtless, emphases. Yet the backbone of the account is, to my memory, true.

No magazine exists without its contributors. To everyone who has appeared in the journal's pages, down the years, whether mentioned or not, my thanks for helping make the Horse what it is.

To our subscribers and supporters, too, my thanks—you know who you are. A special shout-out to Aly Barr for wise counsel down the years, and for knowing the history, and to Misha Snowball.

Lastly, this book would not exist in its current form without the close reading of, and comments on, earlier drafts by our US editors, Marcia Menter and Jennifer Goodrich, as well as my editor at Happen*Stance*, Helena Nelson. My sincere thanks to them and to the book's indexer, Margaret Christie. Any errors, of course, are mine alone.

—GC
Lanarkshire
Scotland
15 July, 2016

The Early Years:

1994–1999

THERE ARE VERY FEW THINGS on which I am a world authority, but the subject of this book is one. This is the story of *The Dark Horse*, a transatlantic poetry magazine which in 2015 celebrated its first twenty years. I have edited it since its beginnings. In the past two decades this little magazine, begun almost on a whim, has made me lasting friendships and enemies, involved me in controversies in distinguished journals such as *The Times Literary Supplement*, taken me numerous times across the Atlantic, and caused me to coolly re-assess, at various points, my own writing. At heart this is a story of personalities, for what is literature but a profoundly human affair?

Little magazines do not obey the normal rules of publishing, one of which is to make money. They have never made anyone rich, though they may have made some publishers a lot poorer. They may begin from high-minded motives, such as 'helping to shape the culture'. Even today, an air of romance, faintly comic buffoonery and Dionysiac energy may still cling to a little magazine of any note, particularly at its outset.

The 'little' only applies to the journal's resources and likely circulation; its ambitions may contrast spectacularly with its probable reach. *Leopardskin Jockstrap, The Staggering Poet, Cloud Puffballs, Emerald Schism, Angry Penguins, Rainbow Explosion*: have you heard of them? I doubt it, as five of those six unlikely monikers are fictitious. I have just made them up. One, however, belonged to a journal famous in its day. It's a measure of the bravura and unexpectedness of the little magazine that only someone knowledgeable in this field could pick the genuine among the fake.

As optimistically profligate as tropical beetles, little magazines can vary from seeming pillars of conservatism with plush production values to badly photocopied rags. They don't exist to 'make a profit'; they exist, like those colourful insects, to go on existing.

* * *

The Dark Horse began, or the first thoughts of it did, in the autumn of 1994. In the early nineties I had been involved in editing another little magazine, *Spectrum*, with the poet Stuart A. Paterson. It was a fairly standard mix of poetry, short fiction, occasional reviews and essays, often interspersed with artwork, all in A4 format. Neither of us had much money or resources, but Stuart had discovered that a part of Kilmarnock, Longpark, in Ayrshire, had been designated an APT—an 'area of priority treatment'. This meant that owing to its deprivation extra facilities were made available for the area's inhabitants.

A resource centre in the APT had the newest Apple computers, on which you could book access time. Stuart had become friends with one of the workers at this resource centre, Mick Higgins, who was intrigued by the exposure to a whole world of poetry and creativity of which he knew nothing. He also liked socialising in the pub we drank in, *The Goldberry Arms* in Kilmarnock. Here we would be joined by other remarkable characters, such as the poet Geoff Cooper who at various points also helped out with the magazine. We would sit, quaffing and planning, surrounded by empty glasses, in clouds of cigarette smoke. (I recall one of us, near the end of a lengthy session, regarding the table, piled high, and observing with a note of sudden realisation, 'This table looks like a—*laboratory*.')

My memory is that on the condition that Stuart set up a local writers' group—North West Writers—access would be made available to the computers to typeset the magazine. I had been introduced to Stuart by a friend, the poet and novelist Sam Gilliland; Stuart later asked me to be involved in editing and producing the journal. It was an unusual alliance. Protestant west of Scotland (him) encountered Catholic west of Scotland (me), though we both had Irish backgrounds. Stuart was a bundle of energy and impulse; a gifted poet in the making. Our personalities were usefully complementary. I would say, for instance, 'Did you know [the poet] Stewart Conn is from Kilmarnock?' Stuart didn't, but next thing he had contacted him and solicited work for the magazine. We had plenty of time, both daily and in terms of our relative youth, though I was seven years his senior to the day. We were both developing as poets, but the magazine introduced complications into that relationship, as little magazines do.

We ended up falling out. Until that happened, though, working on *Spectrum* was for me a very useful learning ground. The early issues were simply duplicated and bound in the resource centre with a plastic binder for a spine, though the magazine later progressed to staples. In however modest a way, there were design decisions to make, layout decisions, editorial decisions. I was entirely ignorant, for all my self-taught poetry knowledge, of that more external dimension to the poetry world. I had never used a computer before.

Early on I simply helped out, then assistant-edited, then co-edited; till finally I edited an issue, number six, myself (see page 14) when Stuart was away working on his own writing. He edited the following number. By that point, though, we were growing incapable of working together, and he took the magazine—which, after all, was his. *Spectrum* would continue, later with smaller page dimensions, until 1997.

* * *

In the summer of 1994 I was awarded a Scottish Arts Council writing bursary. With some of the money I decided to set up my own magazine. I had caught the little magazine publishing virus. I enjoyed the buzz. I enjoyed receiving mail in my relatively isolated caravan. I enjoyed the idea that I, a self-taught Irish peasant one step removed, could take part in that bigger conversation as well as writing my own poetry. My own, doubtless romantic, view is that if one engages in it truly, the world of poetry is like a marvellous island where people of all backgrounds and economic levels and skill sets meet. Or at least this is so for those with a broadly shared aesthetic. All that matters on that island is the quality of the work. It is analogous to a quote I have been unable to corroborate but fondly

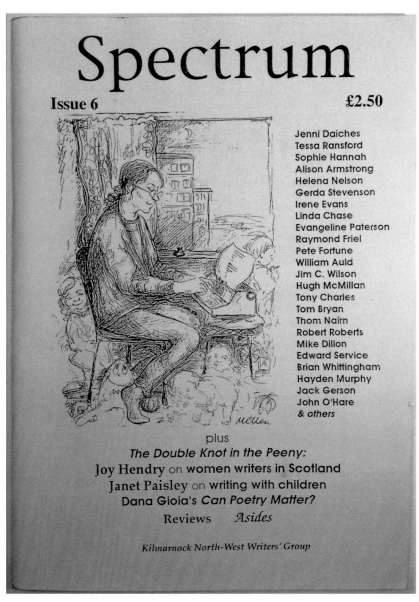

Spectrum

Issue 6   **£2.50**

Jenni Daiches
Tessa Ransford
Sophie Hannah
Alison Armstrong
Helena Nelson
Gerda Stevenson
Irene Evans
Linda Chase
Evangeline Paterson
Raymond Friel
Pete Fortune
William Auld
Jim C. Wilson
Hugh McMillan
Tony Charles
Tom Bryan
Thom Nairn
Robert Roberts
Mike Dillon
Edward Service
Brian Whittingham
Hayden Murphy
Jack Gerson
John O'Hare
& others

plus
The Double Knot in the Peeny:
Joy Hendry on women writers in Scotland
Janet Paisley on writing with children
Dana Gioia's *Can Poetry Matter?*
Reviews   *Asides*

Kilmarnock North-West Writers' Group

Stuart A. Paterson's *Spectrum* was a valuable little magazine, eclectic and dynamic, on the Scottish scene through a good part of the 1990s. It formed a significant component of a little magazine culture in Scotland largely dominated by Joy Hendry's quarterly, *Chapman*, Scotland's most popular literary periodical of the period and among the liveliest of the country's small print journals.

The caravan at Cunninghamhead Estate in Ayrshire where *The Dark Horse* was founded: an icebox in winter, an oven in summer. The photograph at bottom right shows the kitchen table the journal was set up on in the middle distance, also visible in the photograph at bottom left. The typewriter is an Olympia *Traveller De Luxe*, which I still have.

think attributable to Robert Frost (riffing off Tennyson) in response to a lady attending one of his readings: 'I may look like a pauper, madam, but my poems occupy the palace of art.' In those days I looked like a pauper, but I had pride where my own poetry was concerned.

I wrote to Dana Gioia, the American poet-critic, already widely noted on the US literary scene for his 1991 essay in the *Atlantic Monthly* 'Can Poetry Matter?'—an indictment, among other things, of the creative writing industry in the US. I'd become aware of Dana through a special issue about the American New Formalism movement in the poetry magazine *Verse*. My letter mentioned in passing that I was starting up a new magazine of my own. Around ten days later, which was more or less 'by return' in those transatlantic pre-email days, his reply said he'd be willing to be a 'conduit' for work from America provided I made the new magazine 'of more than local interest'. It was a characteristically astute proposition on Dana's part. It provided this US poetry movement with a potential outlet in the UK, however small, both in terms of critical prose and poetry. But it also worked to the—still unnamed—new magazine's advantage. For one, it helped lift the magazine clear of what is often a problem in any small country's literature—parochialism of the worst kind (there is a best kind), nepotism, lack of self-criticism and self-evaluation. And, in its early loose alliance with New Formalism, it helped give the magazine an identity.

New Formalism these days has largely disappeared from view. As I wrote for the *Oxford Encyclopaedia of American Literature*, it

began in the late seventies and early eighties as an informal grouping of younger writers dissatisfied with the prevailing poetry orthodoxy in the [American] Academy. No doubt they felt limited and constrained by an aesthetic there which focused on a subjective, confessional 'I', usually in free verse, and, as young poets of any curiosity at all are likely to, began looking for other models. They found them particularly in the work of poets such as Robert Frost, Robinson Jeffers, and

X. J. Kennedy, writers of wide import who had either kept faith with meter and rhyme or, in Jeffers' case, told stories. These young poets, who included Frederick Turner, Frederick Feirstein, Mark Jarman and Robert McDowell, also grew increasingly aware that poetry had lost its common audience ... and had become a sub-culture, cut off from the life of the mainstream culture and increasingly enervated. They saw the use of meter, rhyme, and narrative as perhaps a way of attempting to address this situation—to escape the ghettoisation of contemporary free verse.

This alliance with New Formalism created a slightly odd disjunction in the magazine in the early days. I have never been a great joiner of 'movements'. I am more likely to attempt to do the opposite of what everyone else is doing. Nonetheless, I found New Formalism engaging because of its focus on form and accessibility as a means of reaching a 'common reader' who had long given up an intelligent interest in poetry and its criticism due to the obscurities of the L=A=N=G=U=A=G=E poets and other elements of the avant-garde. In Scotland, though, and for that matter in Britain, one still to some degree took a common reader for granted. Nor was form politicised as it had been in the US, where its critics allied it, interestingly, with political conservatism. In Britain you wrote in formal or free verse as the fancy took you. The notion of form being *politically* conservative seemed strange—major contemporary poets such as Tony Harrison and Douglas Dunn, politically left-wing, gave the lie to that. (Now, though, their use of the tradition's great forms, given their subject matter, can seem deeply ironic.) The Horse's association with New Formalism, while mostly it worked well, created a dichotomy for the magazine in how it was perceived by the poetry 'community' in Scotland, of which more later. But at that point there were more pressing issues. Such as, for instance, the new journal's name.

* * *

Naming a new poetry magazine, beyond the extravagant titles alluded to earlier, is a significant matter. What will the journal stand for? What, as Ian Hamilton, that doyen of poet-editors, once put it, is its 'project'? Its identity? Its intention? Its aesthetic? People have often asked me where *The Dark Horse*'s name came from. Sometimes I say it was the name of a pub in Kilmarnock (now called *The Hunting Lodge*). Back in *Spectrum* days, Mick Higgins, the resource centre worker who gave us access to computers, perhaps sensed the slight abrasion between Stuart Paterson and me. One afternoon, prompted by the former's enthusiasm and understandable nerviness about access to the equipment, he tried to wind him up by saying, suddenly, 'What was the name of that magazine you were talking about starting, Gerry?' I had been talking about no such thing.

'*The Dark Horse*,' I said, without thinking. Somehow this name remained in the offing when the magazine was being born. Briefly, *The Corncrake* was also a possibility; I liked it, as a lifelong bird person, for its unfashionable unexpected-ness and its pastoral note. Then I began thinking that calling a poetry journal after a rapidly declining and reclusive land rail likely to become extinct in Britain might not be the most auspicious idea. *The Dark Horse*—the outsider, the unknown quantity, the unexpected winner—gradually asserted itself in my mind.

I certainly liked the outsiderness. I was thirty-five. I lived in a caravan. I had never been to university. Owing to my own psychological peculiarities, I was an autodidact in an old Scottish tradition. My attitude was: if you could read, you could educate yourself. (So much for the English Departments of the world's universities.) I'd been attempting this in poetry for, oh, the previous dozen years or so. In a sense, I was *The Dark Horse*'s projected ideal reader. I would make, I must have thought, the magazine I wanted to read. In my shambolic and bumbling fashion, I conceived of the Horse in those days as a larger external simulacrum of my own poetic 'project'—assuming I knew what that was. So, poetry with a 'taste for the genuine', but lit with anarchic energy and humour too. Poetry written out of the full humanity of its speaker. Poetry, as I once wrote hyperbolically in a magazine editorial, aware of the impossibly high standard I was setting, with

> the metrical virtuosity of a Milton, the rhythmical energy of a Jeffers, the radioactive despair of a Larkin, the cranky perfected individuality of a Crowe Ransom or Mackay Brown or Dickinson, the sheer accuracy of an Elizabeth Bishop, the unpredictable idiosyncrasy of a Norman MacCaig, the mysterious playfulness of a Frost, the grievous witnessing of a Zbigniew Herbert, the passion of a Sorley MacLean, or the exuberance and difficult optimism of an Edwin Morgan— ideally, of course. Yet not quite in the manner of these writers. One looks to be surprised by something beyond all of them, something as fresh and wholly itself as a particular light-struck tree, an arrangement of clouds, or a skanky old dog in a city backstreet. One looks for, as Marianne Moore pointed out, and insofar as one can recognise it, what is 'genuine'. But not just that.

I also wanted the magazine to run prose written with some of the virtues of higher journalism as to fact and interest, avoiding the whiff of the academic. My early freelancing for the British *Reader's Digest* magazine between 1983 and 1988, when I was in my twenties, helped. Though it then sold 1.5 million copies a month, I mocked it snootily. (I always chuckled over Stephen King's set-pieces sniping at this mass-market magazine in his novels.) But such journalism's requirement for the readable exposition of even quite complex material had made me impatient of what I call the 'polystyrene chip' school of writing too divorced from any root in the actual.

My model back then for superb critical writing, which doesn't seem so far off the mark even 30 years later, would have been the Randall Jarrell of *Poetry and the Age*. More up to date exemplars, in a different style, might have been the essays and reviews of Ian Hamilton, Dana Gioia, or perhaps Michael Schmidt's *An Introduction to 50 Modern British Poets*—its potted summaries still seem a model of engagement and concision and readability. We weren't talking theory, for god's sake. It wasn't about writing essays to pass exams and achieve high marks in a university context. Not that the writing I envisaged precluded high intelligence, to the extent I could discern it. But I wanted the force of a whole sensibility, with nothing time-serving about it. I wanted it to matter. And what was behind this? That you should stand for what you wrote. That the words you used were significant. I came out of a subservient tradition of respect for authority in which utterance itself was not only unexpected but an achievement. I had always thought my own poetry aimed at reaching a point where I could speak without embarrassment in the poem: a space in which the poem's speaker (whether my autobiographical self or a narrator) fully *occupied* their own words.

In an attempt not to be fooled, to have the highest standards, I brought to submissions a rather severe, truculent, almost begrudging sensibility. I held up each submitted poem, metaphorically, by its corner between finger and thumb as if it were something slightly tainted. The approach then was not the open-hearted generosity recommended in other contexts. It was: *You say you're writing poetry? Okay. Convince me.* Similarly with the criticism. What I asked myself when reading it was: 'Will readers (ie, me) find this interesting? Or is it not fully engaged, merely an exercise?'

Allowances, I think, can be made. Starting a little magazine is a fool's enterprise. So is keeping it going. Such a venture, as I would later write, is 'begot by sheer daftness upon unreasoning optimism'; it 'represents the temporary triumph of idealism over reality.' I had a telephone—it was, after all, 1994—in this caravan, and a radio, but no other technological accoutrements.

The arrival of the postman was a big event in the day. The red postvan passing my window without stopping would leave me quite crestfallen. I had partly begun the magazine to receive mail and thereby offset at least literary loneliness. My then partner, Aileen McIntyre, was opposed to me beginning it at first but once it was obvious that the great wave of impetus would have to be launched upon, and ridden, she warmed to the idea. A woman of formidable intelligence, she was a greatly-valued sounding board and reader of potential contributions for the first ten issues of the journal. I was Scots by adoption but essentially an Irish Catholic by parentage, living in one of the most sectarian parts of Scotland and sharply aware of my outsiderness.

To some extent my retreat to the caravan had been a way of trying to 'work myself out' in a simplified environment before re-entering the world 'to alter with age'. No wonder I was beguiled by episodes like Robert Frost's years of complete obscurity, before his move to England and later acclaim. Emily Dickinson was also one of my guiding spirits. In my twenties I had read her entire corpus one winter and, ignorant of the massive complications of her own background, imagined myself (comically I think now) as a sort of male version of her. Except I could not manage the 'I cannot live with You—it would be Life—' sensibility. I wasn't sufficiently frightened of the sexton's key. I had had my self-scrutinising retreat by that point, and wanted no more of it. Work on *Spectrum* and then on *The Dark Horse* marked the beginning of my emergence from this long, self-imposed darkness.

* * *

Editors & their magazines

The relationship between a little magazine and its editor is intriguing. Some long-lived journals have an identity which is passed on and subtly or radically changed by subsequent editors. London's *Poetry Review*, Chicago's *Poetry*, or Scotland's *Edinburgh Review* are of this type. The new editor takes over the journal but is not its founder.

In other cases, a magazine is inextricably linked with one editor, and is occasionally portrayed as a life's work that saved him (it is usually, in this scenario, a 'he') from what Robert Frost called 'the greater desolations'.

Aquarius, the journal founded, published irregularly, and run from London by Eddie Linden, is of this type. The magazine is positioned as the literary equivalent of a stray dog which the unwitting editor has to rescue and nurture, so saving himself from alcohol and meaningless destitution. It is a story full of charm and optimism, for running a poetry journal successfully has the heartwarming air of all hopeless enterprises undertaken against the odds.

Other poet-editors, however, exist in an ambivalent relationship to the journal they have set up. Even with a bi-annual magazine, the publication becomes a sort of monstrous, giant overlooming child—or in this case, Horse. It perpetually demands large amounts of food, ie content; it stretches the poet-editor's multi-tasking abilities to their limit. No sooner has one issue gone to the printer and been sent out than another has to be planned; the submissions pile up in toppling towers and silently rebuke like a bad conscience, demanding to be read and given thought to; your own poetry, which was why you started the whole enterprise in the first place, is clamouring for attention. Small wonder that a decade is a long life for a little poetry journal. An eloquent precis is supplied by T. S. Eliot. He edited, in its various transmutations, *The Criterion*, later the *New Criterion*, and later still the *Monthly Criterion* (before its quick reversion to a quarterly) through most of the nineteen twenties and thirties. On 12th March, 1923, a year after founding *The Criterion*, Eliot wrote to John Quinn:

> I am now in the midst of a terrific crisis. I wish to heaven I had never taken up *The Criterion*. [...] It has been an evergrowing responsibility ... a great expense to me and I have not got a penny out of it: there is not enough money to run it and pay me too. [...] I think the work and worry have taken 10 years off my life. I have sunk the whole of my strength for the past 18 months into this confounded paper, when I ought to have been minding my own business and doing my own writing. The paper has therefore done me more harm than good. [...] In order to carry on *The Criterion* I have had to neglect not only the writing I ought to be doing but my private affairs of every description which for some time past I have not had a moment to deal with. I have not even time to go to a dentist or to have my hair cut, and at the same time I see *The Criterion* full of the most glaring defects which I could only avoid by having still more time for it to devour.

—from *The Little Magazines: A Study of Six Editors* by Ian Hamilton, London: Weidenfeld and Nicolson, 1976, p70.

Eliot goes on a bit, yet it is all there: the sense of having fathered this time-swallowing insatiable infant (and being fathered by *it*); the sheer anxiety; the hint of craziness about the enterprise; the ambiguity in regard to the journal. I think any poet-editor, in their darkest moments, would recognise this scenario. The self-portrait of a straggle-haired, tooth-achey, high-stressed Eliot overloomed by his *Criterion* has often made me wish I had a caricaturist's gifts.

* * *

Setting up the journal—Dana Gioia—the electronic ruralists

But *this* was the autumn of 1994. A new enterprise was being born. I had plans. Letters between Dana and me crossed the Atlantic with reassuring regularity. He had the *gravitas* and the American connections that I, the shaggy uncultured cara-van dweller with a longstanding interest in American poetry, aspired to. I mean, I was in the sticks in Ayrshire. You fitted together what small pieces of literary life you could.

I was a romantic socialist by long exposure to Scottish cul-ture, tempered by the subconscious hierarchies of my Catholic conditioning. Dana was, as far as I knew, politically conserva-tive. Before his turning freelance as a poet-critic and general man of letters in 1992, he had been a vice-president of General Foods. He was frequently compared to Wallace Stevens as a 'businessman-poet'. There was an air of no-nonsense profes-sionalism about him. This was combined with erudition light-ly worn, a refreshing lack of egomania, and a highly developed sense of the comic. He seemed, in every sense, an achieved spirit. He advised from his business background that I had to get a logo for the journal—something that would instant-ly identify the magazine and what it stood for. 'Of course,' he said, 'it'll have to include a horse. A *dark horse.*'

This was a more complicated task than it seems now in our instant-access online world. In the hunt for an appropriate image I went so far as to commission, for a small sum—£10 or so—a graphic from a local artist. It was not a success. 'Couldn't he have given it longer eyelashes,' Aileen McIntyre said, 'and had it wearing high heels?'

People have often asked me where the image of the Horse for the magazine came from. I based it on a woodcut in an art-book I possessed, reproduced in small format, which somehow I must have scanned or copied to access it electronically. The original was called (not without some irony, I think now) 'The Bewitched Groom', by the Dutch artist Hans Baldung Grün. An enigmatic image created around 1544 and featuring a re-cumbent groom and a horse, it has never been fully explained.

'My' equine was loosely based on a detail from the original. The electronic version was of such poor quality, with numer-ous broken lines, that I had to complete these manually on the computer, effectively making it a new image. What should have been a single graphic ended up having around 30 com-ponent parts. Since I lacked the technical skills to group them together as one, I had to move each part individually every time I changed the position of the horse. This, combined with the slowness of the early computers—the first of which had a 40 megabyte hard disk—made anything using our Horse logo a slow affair. It was years before the indomitable Joe Murray, at that time the publisher/typesetter and editor of Glasgow's *West Coast Magazine* and a very clever and good-spirited man, scanned all these for me as a composite.

Somehow, I had got hold of a computer. It was a secondhand Macintosh SE, one of those early Apple machines that looked like a small grey square television. It had a black and white screen the size of two postcards placed together one above the other. You squinted through this into the ideal world of the fin-ished journal. The computer sat in pride of place on the table-top in the tiny kitchen of my caravan (see page 15). It behaved mercurially at first—sometimes the screen would crackle into broken lines and go blank without warning.

I recall a saga of stressful visits, with the man who sold it to me, to an Apple repair shop on a bleak industrial estate in Glasgow, where they eventually diagnosed the problem as a 'cracked motherboard'. Once it was fixed it worked reliably and the first seven issues of *The Dark Horse*, as well as hundreds of my own poems, were typeset and typed on it using an early version of Aldus *Pagemaker* of dubious origin: the only way to get anything like that done when you had no money.

It was the early days of the desktop publishing revolution. Typesetting, if not quite publishing, from a caravan in the woods had become possible. The poet-critic James McGonigal had coined a phrase for this, and for the likes of me, in an essay: 'the electronic ruralists'.

If I go into *The Dark Horse*'s beginnings in some detail it is to show what was involved. Editors of little magazines are usually general dogsbodies. They don't sit in their ivory towers above the crude or messily creative plains below. They have to develop a range of skills including accounting, typography, design, and editing; a certain amount of psychological acuteness helps too.

* * *

Word got around. Submissions began coming in. Dana suggested an American Assistant Editor, Thomas DePietro, to deal with the journal administratively in the US, send out contributor and subscriber copies, and gather submissions and subscription cheques (or checks). The latter would be grouped and sent to me as a single sum, thus avoiding considerable currency conversion charges on small individual transatlantic cheques in dollars. Submissions began arriving, excitingly with American postmarks, and Dana's substantial letters often included suggestions for poets to contact and essays he believed might be suitable for the journal. It is to his credit that these were seldom more than suggestions, though occasionally they would be strong recommendations. All final decisions on the magazine's content were left to me. (An example of the delicacy of negotiation involved can be seen on page 26.)

Young poets or poet-editors often find or seek out the tutelary spirits they need. In Scotland for me these included the Orkney poet and short story writer George Mackay Brown.

Dana Gioia
7190 Faught Road
Santa Rosa, California 95403

3/15/96

Dear Gerry –

Here is an unpublished poem
by Anthony Hecht. It is quite
marvellously done with all the
Hechtian flourishes. I love the
idea of Proust on ice-skates,
don't you? Let's publish it!
(And if you don't publish it, I
shall be in a difficult situation
since I sweetly coerced it
from him before he had even sent
it out in the U.S.). It will need
to be in the next issue, since it
will appear in a book this fall.

A rare handwritten letter from Dana Gioia. Most of his letters were typed. As can be seen, the final decision on publishing Hecht's poem, 'Proust on Skates' rested with me. The interview by Langdon Hammer with this major poet that Dana mentions is indeed 'superb', well worth looking up for anyone interested in Hecht, whose sestina 'The Book of Yolek' is one of the most powerful poems to come out of the Second World War.

Hecht has provided two footnotes, which you may or may not want to use. I was interested to learn that Proust was fascinated by Vermeer's View of Delft." By the way, I assume that there is a tiny typo or lacuna in the epigraph. I think it _all_ should be italicized.

There is a superb interview with Hecht in the current _Sewanee Review_, which talks about prosody and style inter _alia_. Someone sent me an extra copy which I'll pass on to you.

I'm delighted to have the Hecht. It gives us another _anchor_ for TDH # 3. I felt we were a little light on the big trans-Atlantic names.

Can you send me Wendy Cope's address?

Thanks,

D

The Galloway poet William Neill was another exemplar—writer of some of the best contemporary Scots poetry in the language, and a man who still hasn't been given his literary due.

Dana was hardly a *poetic* influence on me. He had been a precocious youngster brought up in urban Los Angeles. I had been a teenager with an obsession for wild birds and birdnesting used to stravaiging the fields and woods of Ayrshire. We had very different sensibilities, preoccupations and knowledge-sets. As an indication of what a literary life or a life in poetry might be, though, Dana was exemplary. I took great pleasure in receiving his clear typed letters, invariably on white cotton paper folded into white or airmail envelopes with a range of exotic American stamps. Often they would contain clippings or other pieces he thought I would find amusing or interesting. A little poem I wrote at the time, inspired by one such clipping, gives some idea of the dynamic between us:

A TRIOLET EPISTLE/SQUIB

'Gioia Consults Muse
For Poetic Inspiration'—newspaper headline

Gioia Consults the Muse
For poetic inspiration
Too many of us could use.
Gioia Consults the Muse
(Though I must resort to booze
Here in the Scottish Nation).
Gioia Consults the Muse
For poetic inspiration!

So: what chance of her address?
(My liver would be grateful.)
I'd promise to consult her less.
What chance of her address?
Only she, alas, can bless;
The whisky option's hateful.
What chance of her address?
My liver would be grateful!

Now I know that you're well-starred:
The Muse finds you delightful.
Hungover and red-eyed, the truth is hard,
Now I know that you're well-starred,
Her favourite consulting bard;
Me, she finds quite frightful.
Now I know that you're well-starred:
The Muse finds you delightful!

I see you and Euterpe dancing
about the paradisal tree.
Ringed by gazelle and leopard prancing,
I see you and Euterpe dancing,
Consulting (and of course romancing)
With light's perpetual gaiety.
I see you and Euterpe dancing
About the paradisal tree.

There was an element of New York pizzazz and stylishness in Dana's letters that I found, in my relative Ayrshire penury, inspiring and invigorating. There may have been something, too, in his being an Italian-American and a devout Catholic who positioned himself as an outsider and gadfly of the contemporary poetry scene in the US. His advice about, and interest in, the new enterprise was invaluable, even if it did open the magazine to paths it would not have followed had I been left to my own sensibility. Or perhaps especially because it did.

* * *

*The early issues—Number 1—Kirkpatrick Dobie—
the Horse's forebears*

After a winter of planning, issue 1 was published in April 1995. I had chosen an unusual format, B5 (176mm wide by 250mm high), mainly so the journal would appear unique, certainly in Scotland. It was a 56-page saddle-stitched—stapled—production, spineless in only one sense, with a plain cream-coloured card cover. The back cover was blank. A new 'journal of poetry and opinion', as a subtitle on the cover announced, was launched. Dana had taken out some 30 gift subscriptions for poets and critics, mainly in England. This, allied to my own efforts at publicity via a leaflet I had toiled over designing, helped create something of a buzz and response to the inaugural number.

There were no Scottish models for what I intended with the Horse, though *Lines Review* had been the country's most distinguished poetry journal for many years, and I had yet to hear of Ian Hamilton's contentious magazine of the 1960s, *The Review*. Perhaps journals like *The Sewanee Review* or *The Hudson Review*—distinguished major examples of the great tradition of the American little magazine—although with a focus on poetry in the Horse's case, were more what I had in mind. Our first issue's editorial announced itself bumptiously. Its opening paragraph read:

> It is as well to begin by stating what *The Dark Horse* is not. It is not a magazine for partly-achieved work among which the occasional fine poem glints like a diamond; nor is it intended only to be interesting to those who appear in its pages; nor will it feature backslapping and only partially sincere reviews.

(See the complete editorial on page 33.) Those rousing and strident clauses unfolding through successive semi-colons give me a wry smile now. Such editorials in the average little magazine often contrast amusingly with the mediocrity of its contents. Nonetheless, twenty years later, that first issue still seems a respectable performance. It kicked off with a poem by Richard Wilbur which had previously appeared in the *New Yorker*. Dana had encouraged me to occasionally reprint good work from the States which, in pre-internet days, few here would have seen.

The Wilbur poem was followed with a substantial piece by Ann Karkalas on the Dumfries poet and former grain merchant Kirkpatrick Dobie. He had come to my notice when his *Selected Poems*, after a few privately printed pamphlets, had been published by Peterloo Poets—when the poet was 84. With an editor's instinct for a potential 'scoop' I sensed that Dobie might have a good deal of strong unpublished work. I wrote to him and was rewarded with a substantial sampling.

I chose eight poems, which still pass muster. (See 'At Greyfriars', on page 35.) Dobie is far less well known than he should be. You will find him in almost no anthologies of Scottish poetry (though James McGonigal, the poet and later Edwin Morgan biographer, with characteristic percipience included him in one). Dobie's art has both the limitations and the strengths of a parochial sensibility. To a contemporary reader, it can appear at times old-fashioned, particularly in its delicacy around matters such as homosexuality. At core, though, it deals with undateable concerns in the voice of an unusual personality, investigating, probing, and taking nothing for granted. Poetry has traditionally offered a refuge and standing ground for oddballs and obsessives—those who don't fit in or are wonderfully, unpredictably idiosyncratic.

A character such as Dobie embodied what I must have felt, even then, was part of the spirit of the journal. It would take nothing on trust and be chary of the assumed superiority of academe. Dobie had never been to university yet could quote reams of Shakespeare and discuss it in remarkable detail, not based on this or that critical authority, but directly out of his own intellect. It did not matter to me that he was solidly right-wing and loved the Queen. His best poems outwitted his own predilections. He regarded poetry not as an academic subject but as an art thoroughly entwined with the roots of common existence. He brought an untutored and intense innocence to its contemplation. This could be unnerving, because his ego did not seem involved and so he was entirely free to scrutinise or expose the dark corners of your own ignorance.

Dana Gioia and I were represented in the issue in both poems and prose—ostensibly to give a flavour of what we stood for. My own prose was a review of the Scottish poet Tom Scott's *Collected Shorter Poems*. A brief extract will give something of its tenor:

continues on page 38

A Journal of Poetry and Opinion

The Dark Horse

Kirkpatrick Dobie:
an appreciation and eight poems
***

William Neill: *The Power of Form*
***

X. J. Kennedy: *Epigrams*
& an interview
***

Poems: Richard Wilbur, Edwin Morgan,
Anne Stevenson, Iain Crichton Smith
***

Dana Gioia: *On Passion*

No. 1

$5.00   £3.00

The front cover of our inaugural issue, which was basically a large format glorified pamphlet. The austere modesty of such an item, if well typeset, I still find appealing.

Editorial

It is as well to begin by stating what *The Dark Horse* is not. It is not a magazine for partly-achieved work among which the occasional fine poem glints like a diamond; nor is it intended only to be interesting to those who appear in its pages; nor will it feature backslapping and only partially sincere reviews.

The Dark Horse is an international poetry magazine published in Scotland that will set formal poetry at the centre of its aesthetic. It will not be evangelical or doctrinaire, but believes that traditional verse is worthy of more attention than it currently enjoys. A recent anthology of younger Scottish poets, for example, acknowledged Edwin Morgan as its presiding spirit. Morgan, a protean and restless writer, is also a fine formal poet; yet the anthology, non-partisan in other ways, contained little that was recognisably formal.

Of course, writing in traditional forms is no guarantee of excellence in poetry. *The Dark Horse* will not discriminate against compelling free verse, for it is relatively easy to write reams of what Frost called, discouragingly, 'rimey-dimey stuff'; metronomically-regular wooden verse as dull as the most papery language poetry. Yet perhaps not quite. Writing in traditional forms tends to impose upon the poet the need to be, at the least, aurally memorable. It is intended to make each issue of the magazine, as well as a forum for essays, appreciations, and polemics, an anthology of poems which can be read and re-read; poems to move, delight, provoke, intrigue, inspire, enlighten, and involve.

The strident debut editorial of a little magazine is a literary genre in its own right. My own example is relatively mild compared to that, for instance, of Dunstan Thompson's *Vice Versa*, an American poetry magazine of November–December 1940:

> *If the contemporary journals are bad because of their editors, they are worse because of their contributors. Obscene old men, whose reputations are no more than literary—derived from work done far in the past, now vitiated by boredoms of obsessive writing, since they refuse to die with decency, must be put away before their already corruptive mortality becomes too nauseating to be endured. Nor should any mercy be expected by those in the fattening forties who, married to middle age, yet still flirting with adolescence, lack both the achievements of maturity and the promises of youth. As for the golden lads, whether they come with the humous provinciality of the yokel, or the gas-light sophistication of the slicker, they need not think that their sentimentalism, be it from the pig-sty or the ballroom, shall escape the white light of truth that burns with the fire of the phoenix. All, all of them, fakers, frauds, and counterfeits, all of them must be destroyed.*

Why Kirkpatrick is no longer a dark horse in the poetry world

● Dumfries poet Kirkpatrick Dobie with a complimentary copy of the new magazine.

OCTOGENARIAN poet Kirkpatrick Dobie is, by his own admission, barely known outside south-west Scotland.

But that's about to change.

For he features prominently in a new international poetry magazine, The Dark Horse.

It includes a five-page appreciation of his work, eight examples of his poetry and extracts from letters.

Kirkpatrick, aged 87, of Corberry Mews, Dum-

fries, was somewhat surprised by the interest from the publishers.

He said: "It's quite a bolt from the blue, the fact that they have fastened on to someone like myself.

"My position is very odd. I have not come before the public hardly at all, but I have made quite an impression on the literary people that I have come across."

Rather than send his poems to magazines or become part of the poetry reading circuit, he published a number of small pamphlet collections in Dumfries and sold them locally

Until Peterlee Poets brought out a selection in 1992, few outside Dumfries and Galloway knew of his work.

The inclusion in The Dark Horse, self-described as a journal of poetry and opinion, will gain him wider recognition. The magazine is about to go on sale in the UK (priced £3) and America.

For further information contact: Gerry Cambridge, Editor, The Dark Horse, 19 Cunninghamhead Estate, by Kilmarnock, Ayrshire, Scotland KA3 2PY

Kirkie Dobie, wearing his characteristic indoor hat. The press interest shown here was prompted when he sent his local paper a copy of issue 1.

At Greyfriars*

Who now remembers Dr. Weir? I don't.
I got his story from my mother,
how splendidly he preached, how splendid looked,
how he arrived unwed
and all the girls were after him, so keen
that when he did get married, someone made a scene.

Maybe it was inevitable
since he was eloquent
and tall and slim and sanctified.
As such I see him poised, his practised glance
sweeping the congregation like a lighthouse beam.
Chapter and verse I hear him cry
then "Lov'st thou me?" and "Lov'st thou me?" again,
and yet a third time, this time lingeringly. —
And then and shatteringly —
"No! Robert Weir! I hate ye! Hate ye! *Hate ye!*"

Shouting they got her out, and I suppose
that he went on
and later, lost no sleep
out of concern for that one sheep.

Of course, I could be wrong. Perhaps
he left his image by mischance,
a thing that sometimes happens. Perhaps
the clay he worked on was too soft
and 'credulous to false prints' as Shakespeare says.
Perhaps. Perhaps in time he led
legions to life.
I do not know. Only that here
the effect was otherwise.
As if he preached not Christ but Dr. Weir.

* *Greyfriars Church, Dumfries*

The forthright excellence, neatly turned and made, of a Kirkpatrick Dobie poem at its best: formal rigour allied to what is, ultimately, ordinary speech. This is one of eight poems by him from our inaugural issue.

Dana Gioia

22 Hastings Landing • Hastings-on-Hudson • New York • 10706

April 28, 1995

Dear Gerry,

Please don't assume my brief silence on The Dark Horse is disapproval.
The issue arrived only a little over a week ago. The mailman literally
arrived just as I had walked out the door with suitcase in hand to head
down to Washington. I have been on the go ever since--readings, classes,
a TV show, a radio show, two official evenings with literary societies,
in other words all of the time-wasting things society invents to keep
poets from writing. This morning you find me both exhuasted and slightly
depressed by the increasing vapidity of my life.

The Dark Horse looked awfully good, I thought. You have made the
strong debut I had hoped for. I can't seem to find my only
copy. It is lost somewhere in the squalor of my study. I think I
can reconstruct most of it from memory, however.

The key strengths of the issue were: 1)Professionalism--all the time
and effort of planning the magazine showed in its format and style;
2) Substance--your first issue was clearly not just another small magazine;
it had depth and heft, real authors with real work; 3)Variety--the mixture
of poems, essays, reviews, and the interview made a broad appeal to
literary readers; 5) Quality--the contents were worth reading.

What did I think were the best things in the journal? Probably
the poems by Wilbur, Stevenson, Kennedy, Gwynn, Mason, Morgan, and
Graham. (I pass no judgment on you and me, for obvious reasons, but I
will point out that it was good for both of us to have poems in the
first issue to mark our commitment.) I also liked the Helena Nelson
poem, though I'm not altogether sure I understood it. I liked the
whole Kirkpatrick Dobie feature, though you might have been a bit more
selective on the letters you quoted. (Perhaps, though, that informality
is just what you want.) The Kennedy interview is good and contentious.
I liked what A. B. Jackson was trying to do more than how well he
succeeded. I was most disappointed in the Neill essay. It meandered,
and its point was essentially "form isn't bad." I'm glad to have Neill
writing prose for our first issue, but I don't think we need any more
defenses of form on such a level. We can be more assertive and specific.
We can assume that form isn't too bad. The reviews are thin--not bad,
just not enough of them. Your piece on Scott was fine. Your lead
was especially helpful to an American; it placed Scott for us.

All in all, an estimable beginning. The Dark Horse has established
its seriousness and discernment. Now we need to keep getting better.
Here are some ideas:

1) Use the back cover--either sell or trade an ad with some other
journal or feature some article or articles contained in the issue.
The back cover is the second most prominent place in the journal. Don't
waste it. That is a sure sign of an amateur journal.

2) <u>Commission some good reviews</u>: I think that we should praise excellence and blow the whistle on influential crap. We don't really have the room to do everything in between. We can't really cover the poetry scene, not even in Scotland. I would suggest that we review the 1 or 2 most important new Scottish books and then run 2-3 more short(1 or 2 pages) reviews with a strong point-of-view of significant American books. A dozen or so pages of strong reviews will give the journal authority. We might consider going a bit longer for the next issue. 64 pages? You should write Robert McPhillips and ask him to do a review of some new American book. Shall I ask him and select some volume. Tom DePietro will also be good. He is a tough and smart fiction reviewer for <u>Kirkus Review</u> where all reviewers write anonymously. Since Tom is outside the poetry subculture, he reviews honestly. That is a huge advantage for us. (I shall insert a xerox of his Disch reivew with this letter.)

3) <u>Get some good essays</u>. We have talked about this. There are 36 people reading papers in West Chester. I shall try to find something publishable there next month.

4) <u>A terrific interview</u>: This is probably our most pressing need. I will mull it over. Could we convince Bill Rice to interview somebody else? Do you think we could get somebody to interview James Fenton or Wendy Cope? What about Edwin Morgan? Maybe a short interview with a younger American? I think that interviews add a human element that the journal should cultivate. It keeps things from getting too academic or stuffy.

   I am pleased to know there is a possiblility of our dark stallion feeding at the public trough. Support will come if the journal becomes outstandingly good. We need to keep prominent American names in the magazine--not merely for Stateside readers but especially for the Scots. It will remind them that ours is different from all other Scottish journals.

All the best and congratulations on TDH 1,

A typical letter from Dana about the magazine in the early days. A mix of suggestion, advice, and personal detail, this was his response to our launch issue.

The negative side of a poetry of conviction is that it can harden into dogma. At his worst, Scott gives vent to cries of rage and shame at the state of the world. These are obviously sincere, but in their failure as poetry they remind one of the bleak wisdom of Donald Davie's 'By the end of the third stanza / death is a smell no longer; / it is a problem of style'.

The issue also contained a spirited interview with Joe (X. J.) Kennedy, an Irish-German American who had been writing in rhyme and metre for decades. An Old Formalist, his poetry crossed its formality with an often anarchic sensibility, particularly in sexual matters (see his 'The Flagellant's Love Song' with its rousing 'Hooray, the birch bark's thwacking!') There was very much a sense of the magazine finding its feet. 'All in all,' wrote Dana from New York, 'an estimable beginning. Now we need to keep getting better.'

* * *

Issue 2—the bumptious animal—Thomas M. Disch &
reviewing—poetry scoops—poets & reputations—
William Neill & Timothy Murphy

By issue 2, which appeared in late autumn 1995, with the same colour of cream card and cover design, the magazine had bulked up to 72pp. The note of polemic and protest was more robust. I had opted to travel to Winchester in the south of England on the day I was supposed to begin an HNC course in Desktop Publishing at the Glasgow College of Building and Printing. My purpose was to interview Wendy Cope—a decision that showed where my priorities lay. Cope's bestselling *Making Cocoa for Kingsley Amis* had broken out of the enclosed world of poetry into a wider readership. She was greatly admired by a number of the New Formalist Americans.

The issue also ran an intriguing exchange of letters between Richard Wilbur and the *New Yorker*, contesting the use of the word 'irradiated'. Dana had unearthed the correspondence in the voluminous manuscript resource of the Berg Collection in the New York Public Library. The letters were witty and lively albeit with a tone of gentility. In an introduction the Berg's archivist Rodney Phillips described the correspondence as 'enchanting and educational about poetry and publishing, and eventually about life, or how to take things firmly but lightly...' Such phrasings struck a note a touch too *Reader's Digest*-y for the extremisms of a Scottish literary temperament, which has been characterised by the 'Caledonian Antisyzygy': a grinning gargoyle kneeling by a saint. Yet I also found this element of New York high style pleasing in its graciousness.

Issue 2's editorial continued more forcefully and comically the tone of high-handed bumptiousness begun with issue 1:

> *The Dark Horse* believes in the meritocracy of craftsmanship. Let us not discriminate against learned poetry. But neither let us fall into the trap of thinking a poem modest in cultural baggage is necessarily inferior. Let me speak up, as a reader, for poems modest in this way. There is too much talk about 'the great' in poetry. Yeats, for instance, is commonly instanced as among the greatest of modern poets. Dylan Thomas said that he thought Yeats *was* the greatest poet; but that it was *Hardy's* poetry which he loved reading. Frost, like the W. S. Graham of poems such as 'Enter a Cloud' is 'great', to this reader, for the examination of things under his nose, reminding of that rabbi who, when asked why most people nowadays couldn't see God, replied, 'Because most people these days can't stoop low enough.'

A little magazine thrives on a sense of personality. My editorial tone in the early numbers was affected in the manner of a young person trying out various styles of handwriting as he negotiates his personality. I was rapidly learning that the contents of a journal were not wholly a reflection of one editor's character and opinions. The only way to fulfil that impossible outcome would be to write the entire magazine oneself. Nonetheless, re-reading this issue I still find it sparky, barbed in places and interestingly polemic. In writers of the prose, I had chosen critics who accorded with my description of Kirkpatrick Dobie—opinionated and idiosyncratic, but knowledgeable enough for their opinions to carry weight. Dana had previously primed me about a piece he thought would be a scoop, if I 'had the balls for it.' This macho appeal to my masculinity was hardly to be ignored, even though I was quite aware I was being 'set up'. I responded with a squib uncharacteristic of me or my seriousnessness:

> Has Cambridge *balls?*
> Has Glencoe *waterfalls?*
> Has New York *shopping malls?*
> So, before he lose 'em,
> He should use 'em!

The 'scoop' was by the science fiction novelist and poet who wrote as Thomas M. Disch in prose and Tom Disch in poetry. 'The Bonfire of the Vanities: Poetry Reviewing in America' was a personal and forthright account of his own experiences as a poetry reviewer. Here are its opening paragraphs:

> There is a good reason most reviews of poetry are so dull, and it's not just because the same can be said for most poetry. It's true that review editors tend to assign the books of dull poets to critics of congruent dullness, but even zany poets are likely to inspire dull reviews.
>
> The reason is this: poets are regarded as handicapped writers whose work must be treated with a tender condescension, such as one accords the athletic achievements of basketball players confined to wheelchairs. Poets don't make the best-seller lists; they don't expect to earn a living from their poetry. Their jobs at the fringe of a bloated educational bureaucracy benefit neither the larger economy nor the little commonweal of poetry. Rather, like other forms of 'special education', poetry workshops exist to foster a self-esteem that, in its fullest flower, verges on delusions of reference.
>
> The woeful 'marginalisation' of poets has nowhere been celebrated with more heartfelt self-pity or greater conviction of self-righteousness than by Adrienne Rich in her book-length

manifesto, *What Is Found There* (Norton, 1993). 'Poets in the United States,' she writes, 'have either some kind of private means, have held full-time, consuming jobs, or have chosen to work in low-paying, part-time sectors of the economy...' Indeed; and what options does that omit? Only dereliction, crime, and prison. In addition to having to earn a living, poets have also to contend with 'the shrinkage of arts funding, the censorship-by-clique, the censorship of the Right, the censorship by distribution.' Add all these forms of hardship and censorship together and the grim outlook is this: *some poets may not be published!*

    Rich's sense of entitlement is unusual only in her having given it expression at book length...

While there may be plenty to disagree with here, Disch's plain speaking is as exhilarating as it may be discomfiting. Much of what he says is relevant today, though even then I cavilled at the 'handicapped' reference. (Dennis O'Driscoll would later call Disch 'notorious' in his polemical style.) Even in its more provocative aspects, though, it's a far cry in its polemicism from the satire which Ian Hamilton published in *The Review*. That had verged on the actionable.

    Someone—probably Dana—had given me the contact address for the Australian poet A. D. Hope; the old poet was bedridden by that point, but in response to my letter had instructed his son to let me publish, via his agent, three poems. I chose two for issue 2; the third followed in *The Dark Horse* 3. Donald Davie, responding to a complimentary copy of issue 1, responded by submitting four poems, a subscription, and an offer to 'help out' if the venture got into financial difficulties. It was a kindness at odds with his reputation as truculent, reactionary and grudging. (See page 64.) I chose one poem. By the time it appeared, he had died.

    I felt I had two other poetry scoops in the issue. One was William Neill's rendering in fluent Scots, 'lipper wi smeddum and virr ('full of pith and virility'), of an extract from the Irish poet Brian Merriman's magnificent, excoriating, 17th-century poem 'The Midnight Court'. Neill's note to his extract read:

[Merriman's] poem is remarkable in being a truly 'European' poem in Irish Gaelic, a break with tradition, dealing as it does with social issues and sexual mores concerning the country poor of Merriman's Ireland rather than aristocrats and legend. In the Ireland of the time it was common to find poor young women married to rich old men, and rich old women married to young men, by the compulsion of economic circumstance. The effect of this on rural polity is the theme of Merriman's poem.

Neill as a native Scots speaker had in Scots a deftness reminiscent of MacDiarmid or Garioch which was uncommon among younger generations of writers in that tongue. To write sustained four-beat rhyming couplets of such eel-like sinuosity as these is no mean feat technically:

She wadna yelloch an skirl an scrat	*scream, screech, claw*
or tak the gate lik a scaddit cat	*make off, scalded*
but streikit oot wi a richt guid will	*stretched out*
stridlegs, an gleg an howpfu still	*astride, lively, hopeful*
fleetchin his thochts wi monie a hint	*coaxing*
mooth ti mooth wi this daud o flint;	*lump*
an amorous tae on his cauld hide prokin,	*toe, cold, poking*
frae his painch ti's thie she preised her mawkin...	*belly, thigh*
	pressed,
	maidenhair

Why is William Neill not better known? A poetic reputation is constructed of various components: quality of the work; perception of the poet as a personality; a talent for self-promotion; and, in some measure, luck.

As a younger man, Willie had alienated many influential literary people in Scotland both by his plain speaking and his political nationalism which had been condensed by his detractors into a crudely simplistic, tub-thumping, kilt-wearing Anglophobia. (When I knew him, he was anything but; for one, his wife, 'Dodo', was a home counties bluestocking.) When fulminating in this mode he had been called by Norman MacCaig to his face, according to the Edinburgh poet and former merchant seaman Stanley Roger Green, 'a palpitating marshmal-low'. 'Pretty deadly', said Green, 'when you think about it'.

I recall George Mackay Brown offering to send me a copy of Willie's *Selected Poems* he'd been sent by his publisher—a sure sign in that subtle and understated man of his disdain. Per-haps if I'd known Willie in his earlier days, like George, who must have encountered him around the Rose Street bars in Edinburgh in the 1960s, I'd have felt similarly.

Another reason for Willie's neglect is that there has been no rigorous *Selected Poems* to stand as a lasting monument. This is complicated by his writing in Scots and Gaelic as well as English. But a slim book of even his best work in Scots would be a significant volume. Considering its sheer variety, I later wrote of his output:

> If the verse written by a poet was a party, some such parties would have only one or two people as guests. Neill's party, on the other hand, would be thrang with solitaries, genteel lady recluses, retired seadogs; once-handsome soldiers with their legs blown off would be pushed in in wheelchairs; old farmers and their canny and resentful women would stand in separate groups; lovelorn young men would be shaking their heads at their fathers' wise but dull advice; there would be a gathering of rich lascivious artisans, of old poets, of rancorous and jeal-ous poets; Rimbaud would rub shoulders with Emily Dickin-son, a millman with a hook for a hand would be frightening a child, a skull would be talking to a man, English Lords would chew on their moustaches...

Perhaps his work will be returned to in the new climate of cultural self-determination fostered by the Scottish Independ-ence debate and referendum of September 2014.

Any poet-editor of a little magazine lives in hopes of a dis-covery. Another of issue 2's major contributions came from a poet that the fine poet-critic David Mason, then teaching in Minneapolis, had put me in touch with: Timothy Murphy. At that point Murphy had been writing for twenty years without trying to publish anything. He was then a venture capital-ist and, on paper at least, a rich man. He liked to glamorise himself as a farmer-poet like Robert Frost. He *was*, though, a hunter, and right-wing gay Catholic alcoholic living in Fargo with his partner, Alan Sullivan. He had studied at Yale under Robert Penn Warren. He sent me an entire manuscript from which to select poems if I wanted any.

In April of that year, 1995, he also wrote to me and asked what would be the 'minimum financial assistance' I would need to attend the inaugural West Chester Poetry Conference in Pennsylvania, strongly associated with New Formalism. I had no idea. At that point a transatlantic flight seemed to me as unlikely as a trip to the moon. I replied, '$500.' He sent a cheque for this amount.

In the meantime, though, I had had second thoughts, fearing my editorial independence would be compromised. I returned the cheque. But I still chose three poems of Murphy's for issue 2. All his work is strongly influenced by Yeats and Frost—his literary genealogy is relatively straightforward—and rigorously metred and frequently rhymed or slant-rhymed. While it generally strikes a graver note, it can also have a wry, comedic aspect. Here, for instance, is 'Deconstruction' entire:

> Rummaging in rubble
> critics are scribbling
> like fieldmice nibbling
> in a farmer's stubble.

A squib, yes, but also a piece of implicit and memorable literary criticism in four lines. Riffing on his own background, however romanticised, it returns power to the poet: the great harvest is taken in, for elsewhere. The critics are ancillary to the primary energy of creation. The mice are comic in their nibbling and purely subsidiary to the process from which they benefit.

Issue 2 also published Murphy's bleak, beautiful performance in assonance and processional despair, 'Harvest of Sorrows'. It is worth reproducing as it first appeared in the journal (see page 46).

══════════ *A Journal of Poetry and Opinion* ══════════

The Dark Horse

Wendy Cope | *Two Poems & an Interview*

Thomas M. Disch | *Bonfire of the Reviews*

A.D. Hope | *Appreciation & Two Poems*

Richard Wilbur | *Autonomy of the Poet*

Dana Gioia | *On a Forgotten Master*

Poems:

George Mackay Brown, Donald Davie,

Gavin Ewart, Donald Justice, X. J. Kennedy

No. 2

$5.00   £3.00

A highlight of issue 2 was a deeply personal interview with Wendy Cope, whom I'd travelled to Winchester in Hampshire to interview in September, 1995. I was also delighted to publish George Mackay Brown's 'Sea Witch', a poem in five sections about Bessie Millie, the 19th century 'seller of winds' from Stromness in Orkney.

Harvest of Sorrows
for Kelly Miller

When swift brown swallows
return to their burrows
and diamond willows
leaf in the hollows,
when barrows wallow
and brood sows farrow,
we sow the black furrows
behind our green harrows.

When willows yellow
in the windy hollows,
we butcher the barrows
and fallow the prairies.
The silo swallows
a harvest of sorrows;
the ploughshare buries
a farmer's worries.

Now harried sparrows
forage in furrows.
Lashing the willows,
the north wind bellows
while farmers borrow
on unborn barrows.
Tomorrow, tomorrow
the sows will farrow.

Note: a barrow is a castrated pig

One of Timothy Murphy's, for my money, finest early poems, also a favourite of Richard Wilbur's: a small masterclass of processional grief and assonance in dimeters.

Somewhere between issue 2 and issue 3, in spring 1996, I was in Kilmarnock one day. I read, in a short-lived literary magazine called *Words* which had somehow managed distribution via the magazine racks of W. H. Smith's newsagents, a remarkable piece on the American poet Robert Lowell. Whoever its author was, his knowledge on the poet was impressive. I turned to the author credit: Philip Hobsbaum.

I vaguely knew of Hobsbaum via 'The Group' and the 'Belfast Group' that Seamus Heaney had attended. I had been unaware that, as the biographical note indicated, he now lived and taught just up the road in Glasgow. Somehow I got hold of his address at the university, and sent him copies of the Horse and my own first book *The Shell House*, which had appeared in July 1995. Back came an invitation to visit him.

One afternoon I found his office among the distinguished cloisters and was invited in, much to the excitement of his spaniel, and instructed to sit in an armchair under what appeared suspiciously like an interrogation lamp. He said, in commanding Patrician tones, 'Now, tell me *all* about yourself.' Such an immediate expectation of intimacy and revelation with someone I'd never met before wrong-footed me a touch, as perhaps it was meant to, but I must have passed whatever test had been set: from this first meeting followed a long, occasionally rocky association until Philip's death a decade later.

A few years after that first meeting he retired, and I would visit him in the book-packed house in Glasgow's west end shared with his wife Rosemary, an impressively well-read woman—she seemed at least as literary as Philip.

Such meetings would follow a typical pattern: Philip would answer the door with an expression somewhere between suspicion and scrutiny; on ascertaining your identity, he would say 'Ah, it's you!' and you would be invited in.

He cut a tubby, markedly pear-shaped, shuffling-in-slippers figure. He would usher you to the living room where you would be offered wine or whisky as a matter of course. He no longer drank whisky himself owing to his diabetes, but had been given a crate of *Macallan* fine malt as part of the honorarium for judging a short story award sponsored by that selfsame distiller. Whisky-loving visitors would be treated to wineglass-sized servings of this vintage tipple.

Conversation, on this or that matter of current interest, though he tended to monologue, would begin. If you had a book for him, this would be examined intently, his spectacles pushed back onto his upper forehead, the volume held a few inches in front of his face—he suffered from poor eyesight all his life. His conversational style was professorial, didactic, loud, and sprinkled with words like 'desuetude', the whole de-livered at high speed.

He had by this time replaced his first, much-loved span-iel, which had died, with another almost identical dog. There were, however, personality differences with this second pet. If Philip's wife was out, the dog behaved territorially.

On one occasion, as the professor rose from the armchair in his living room, the animal responded by crouching as if to leap for his throat, with a low, to-be-taken-*very*-seriously, growl. 'Gerry,' he said, slowly descending back into his arm-chair when faced down by this domestic Cerberus, 'would you mind fetching us another bottle of Chardonnay from the fridge in the kitchen? You see how appalling the situation is: I, a distinguished Emeritus Professor from a major European University, am now not even permitted to leave my armchair and visit my own kitchen because of intimidation by this in-fernal creature!'

Quickly into our friendship I realised that, in a long literary life, Philip had known many of the significant figures in post-war British poetry. I also perceived him to be fearless in his critical views, unlikely to be intimidated or unduly impressed by the reputations of writers then in vogue. I considered him, albeit with complications, as a sort of massive and hugely knowledgeable critical Rottweiler. In a poetry culture tram-melled by reputation-mindful poets reviewing one another, he could be relied on to say what he thought.

The contemporary poetry scene is a magic forest of associa-tions, favours given and received, friendships and alliances, all of these invisible to the common reader outwith the 'scene' but inevitably affecting what is reviewed, praised, promoted and prized. This produces an, at-times, Emperor's new clothes scenario. So I asked Philip to do occasional reviews of books I felt needed straight speaking. At least as interesting, though, were a series of reminiscences—of Ted Hughes (and Plath) at Cambridge, Patrick Kavanagh in Dublin, and Peter Redgrove, one of Philip's close friends and, in his eyes, a major poet.

With his Polish Jewish emigré ancestry Philip seemed in his own way even more of an outsider than I was. The outsider had taken over the citadel, as often happens. It was the 'Let's occupy yer lousy leasehold, poetry!' syndrome, as Tony Harrison puts it. Perhaps we met in that element of estrangement, though our relationship was not altogether easy. He would mock me with what I took as affection in part because it was so outrageous.

Listening to me about one or other dire affair of the heart, he would say things like: 'Gerry, how on *earth* can you expect to keep a woman? You have no property, you have no degree, you have no financial resources, you don't even have a driving licence!' Yet he also recommended me as a writer to Jay Parini, the American poet, critic, novelist and biographer, who in 2000 was commissioning hefty and lucrative essays for Scribners & Sons and, later, for the *Oxford Encyclopaedia of American Literature*. Over a number of years I contributed a dozen lengthy essays to the former, and in summer 2002 ten essays to the latter.

One of them was on that extraordinary figure, the 19th century poet Jones Very, a particular interest of Philip's. For some reason I could not obtain a credit card to buy the *Collected* Jones Very online from the US. I managed to persuade Philip to lend me his copy, on strict condition I return it by a set date. 'I do hope you realise what a reluctant mark of trust and respect this is on my part,' he said.

When I was late in returning it, he said, 'My book! My book! You scoundrel! Gerry, never tell me you're not Irish. *You* can't get a credit card, so *I* have to do without my Jones Very!' I occasionally made, in my fashion, peremptory statements which would outrage him or which he would take with an unnerving literalness. Once I said to him, confident of agreement, 'Of course, all literary folk have to be at least a little bit mad.'

'Are you calling me *mad?* In a long life not only have I had a distinguished teaching career but I have written some 800 articles and essays for periodicals, as well as numerous books of criticism and poetry. You don't think I could have done all that had I not been entirely *sane*, do you?'

On another occasion I wrote to him, with a blithe ignorance that now makes me wince, that *of course* most literary criticism and reviewing was really only a higher form of copy-editing. I was, I continued, much more interested in *why* a particular critic thought something than in *what* they thought. Back as swiftly as a sparrowhawk into a wood-edge of goldfinches came his scribbled postcard. It read:

> Dear Gerry,
>
> You are a literary amateur, and the reason you think there is no such thing as a literary education is because you have not had one. I am perfectly aware of the topic you alluded to: it formed the subject of my PhD, later published as *A Theory of Communication*. Read that book, sometime!

Anyone in the literary arts who lives long enough will find themselves patronised by their juniors who, caught up by the alluring crackle of the present, have no idea of the depth and range of their elders' knowledge.

* * *

With his wife Rosemary, Professor Philip Hobsbaum in his spacious house in Glasgow's west end scrutinises a student's poems, sometime in the summer of 2001. Young poets I took to visit him included Jen Hadfield, Cheryl Follon, and Charu Suri who is now a travel writer for publications such as the *New York Times.*

Sometime around then I'd become interested in Ian Hamilton, the poet, critic and editor. I had known of his minimalist lyric poems, which failed to impress me at the time—I think much more highly of them now—but not his editing. In the sixties and early seventies he had edited *The Review*. It was a polemical poetry journal whose tutelary spirit had been Al Alvarez, in opposition to Michael Schmidt's *Poetry Nation*, now *PN Review*, in which the same role was taken by Donald Davie. (The inagural number of *The Review* featured Alvarez interviewing Davie.) In the seventies Hamilton had moved on to found and edit *The New Review*, a literary magazine with a wider remit. He agreed to an interview with me, which took place at his house in Wimbledon at Easter, 1996.

In those days I often used alcohol to steady my nerves. I had already had three drinks before I rang his housebell, and the door was opened by two of his young sons, both excited, it seemed, to have a visitor.

Hamilton was waiting for me on the first landing of the staircase. He was more diffident, indeed nervous, than I expected for such a prominent literary figure, and had a dry, rather clipped, Oxbridge accent. The first part of the interview took place in his study at a table on which sat a manual typewriter. The conversation was occasionally interrupted by one or other of his sons, with whom he displayed a demeanour of mildly exasperated indulgent affection.

I had brought as a gift a bottle of *Glenfiddich*. Perhaps observing my own nervousness, he cracked this open, though he took only a token measure—it was just 11am, after all—compared to mine. I knew, by that time, a good deal about him, particularly his early editing career, as I think he quickly surmised; perhaps it was an indication of how well the interview was going that he suggested lunch at a nearby Italian restaurant. Accompanied by his sons, we continued over food and two bottles of wine. The interview, as it became more relaxed and unbuttoned in the increasingly busy restaurant, also became more difficult to transcribe later from the cassette of my primitive recorder. A lifelong football fan, he tried during the later stages of lunch to engage me in discussion about the sport. I told him as a youngster I'd had a fondness for Leeds United, largely based on the then pure white of the team's football strip. 'Very aesthetic,' he said.

It was the only time we would meet. Afterwards, wandering about in the Wimbledon Easter sunshine, I felt happy—I knew I had something good. (Ahdaf Soueif, the Egyptian novelist and the mother of the two boys, later told me Ian had been 'taken by surprise' by the interview.) Twenty years later, our conversation—wide-ranging, open, dealing with the nuts and bolts of little magazines, one's own relation as a poet to one's editing, and so on—remains one of the things I am proudest of in the history of the journal. Alan Jenkins, who edited Hamilton's *Collected Poems* for Faber in 2009, quoted from it extensively in that book's introduction.

When I attended a memorial event for Hamilton in Oxford at his College, Keble, in November 2014, his brother spoke about the interview warmly as one of the best of such pieces he'd come across, though Ian himself felt parts of it were 'pretty embarrassing'. I had to reassure him by sending him a list of reader responses.

As is often the way, Ian had no complete run of back issues of *The Review*, but I came away from our meeting with copies of issue 1 and 2 of this plain, card-covered production—very much, indeed, as the Horse was in those days. He also gifted me a signed copy of his first pamphlet (see pages 54 and 55). Issue 1 of *The Review* I kept; I sent issue 2 to Dana. But *The Review* had been edited by an Oxford graduate who had the aesthetic confidence to regard his magazine as culturally central and potentially influencing taste. I was an outsider who had no such confidence and indeed regarded the whole notion of influencing anybody as suspect.

* * *

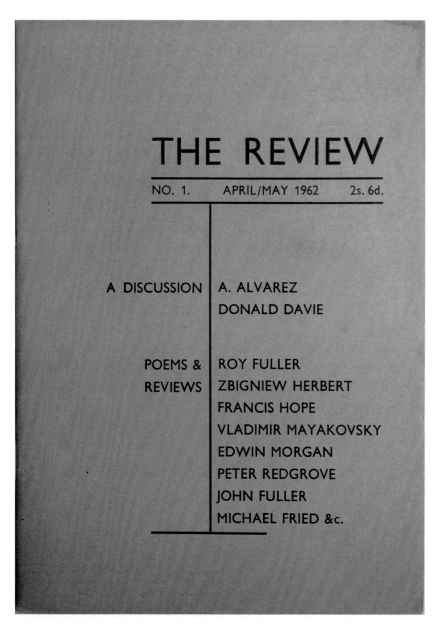

THE REVIEW

NO. 1.   APRIL/MAY 1962   2s. 6d.

A DISCUSSION | A. ALVAREZ
DONALD DAVIE

POEMS & | ROY FULLER
REVIEWS | ZBIGNIEW HERBERT
FRANCIS HOPE
VLADIMIR MAYAKOVSKY
EDWIN MORGAN
PETER REDGROVE
JOHN FULLER
MICHAEL FRIED &c.

A new literary venture with, as Norman MacCaig had it, 'the purity of all beginnings.' Ian Hamilton's *The Review*, an A5 publication set in a sans serif—Gill Sans, I believe.

Opposite: the cover of Hamilton's first pamphlet, and his postcard response in his characteristic miniature script to a copy of issue 3 I sent him of the Horse, containing his interview. He writes: *'Thanks for the mag—a good issue, though some of my "interview" was pretty embarrassing. Thanks also for the poems—which I liked, some more than others. But maybe we can discuss them one day, if you ever find yourself in this part of the world.'* I never did, during his lifetime.

the Review

PAMPHLET SERIES No. 3   1s. 0d.

Pretending
Not
To Sleep

Poems by

Ian Hamilton

54 QUEENS ROAD LONDON SW19 8LR

I had forgotten till recently how much interest and animus, as with *The Review*, those early numbers of the Horse attracted. In those offline days, hard copy was the only manifestation of a literary journal. Bar a phone call, a letter was the only way of responding. I filed these responses, issue by issue, in large manila envelopes. The consensus on issue 1 was almost entirely positive. Issue 2 had a stronger polemical stance and generated a like reaction.

To an extent these responses were split down national lines. Some Scots complainants resembled a small gathering of presbyterian grannies and aunts grimly prognosticating on a wayward granddaughter's party taste for mini skirts and high heels; the American, English and Irish respondents were almost exclusively positive and open-hearted. A couple of anonymised examples from the Scots side will suffice:

> What worries me is that the values DH stands for editorially don't seem to be reflected in the verse. As I understand it, the magazine was meant to be a celebration of quality as well as craftsmanship. Please explain to me how ['x'] by [x] fits into this—it is crass, unbearably couthy, + reminds me of something produced at a Woman's Rural Institute writing workshop. This *is* a poem 'modest in cultural baggage', but it is also pish, and not even mildly amusing.

Or this:

> I tried to phone this morning as it would have been easier to talk. I feel it is difficult to know *where to begin* because *we don't seem to be communicating*: ie, you don't seem to have a clue as to what I'm saying or trying to say about my poetry!! I can't go into the depth of explanation required, so this is just brief to say *we'd better meet.*
> [...]
>   I say [all] this because I feel frustrated by your 'arrival' on the scene & *pontification* about form *without seeming aware*

of others who've been working in refined ways for over 25 years in this field!

One well-known Scottish poet went to the trouble of writing a two-page, typed, single-spaced negative critique of almost everything he thought the journal stood for.

I was, I recall, quite sanguine about these responses. For one, I am of the Blakean school which has it that 'disagreement is true friendship'. Also, there were plenty of reactions which were more encouraging. Further, I had the pragmatic self-assurance that I was actually publishing and editing the magazine. Never having done such a thing themselves, such complainants, to me, resembled Roman Catholic priests attempting to advise on the minutiae of sex within marriage. Their views could be considered in that context.

A common complaint was that the material in the journal wasn't living up to my editorial position regarding exemplary standards. It is a frequent assumption among those who have never edited a little magazine that not achieving this is a sign of failure but, in truth, no editor ever does. For one, the submissions don't measure up. Obtaining excellent work for a little magazine, particularly in its early days, is not easy. Not everything, poetry-wise, is going to be of the first water.

Little magazines exist in an interesting relation to some of the 'big names' of poetry who may, understandably enough, be producing the most estimable writing. This applies particularly in the magazine's infancy. At a certain point in a poet's reputation or fame, a poetry magazine needs the poet more than the poet needs the magazine. Names can help generate excitement and buzz around a journal, even where the work by those names is not their best. Readers like to follow the new output of an admired writer.

Insofar as a little magazine ever has truck with commercialism, attempting to increase sales, or attract attention or literary heft, by publishing 'name' poets is as far as it goes. Writers starting to publish often complain that their rejected work is as good as that of x, y or z (insert famous name) in a particular issue. It probably isn't, but assuming it is, for argument's sake, 'as good as' is not good *enough*. It has to be *better*.

To have established sufficient profile for your name itself to generate interest from a readership, even in the modest terms of contemporary poetry, is itself an achievement. The Horse's strategy in the early days was to anchor the issue with some bigger names and publish whatever other outstanding work I could find. Editors always love discoveries. A poet of real talent, who has been writing solidly in obscurity for twenty or thirty years and suddenly approaches your journal because they admire it, is every poetry editor's dream.

The stature of a journal is more easily established by the quality of its critical prose. Good prose is underestimated: in a little magazine its interest and attractiveness may well be less contingent on a 'name' writer, and more on its subject and evident quality, than is the case with that magazine's poetry.

* * *

Issue 3 must have appeared around May of 1996. It had a blue card cover, but otherwise shared the same design template of issues 1 and 2. It was the last Horse to be saddle-stitched. From issue 4, aided by a small Scottish Arts Council grant—in those days, you were eligible to apply for funding for a journal once you had produced two issues unassisted—the Horse evolved a spine. The extra money meant we could afford to have the magazine properly—that is, lithographically—printed. Numbers 1 to 3 had been produced on an enormous glorified photocopier by a London printer, Roger Cullingham.

Meanwhile, with issue 3, problems had arisen with our US Assistant Editor in New York, Thomas DePietro. Owing to some personal difficulties, he had stopped responding to contact from me. My increasingly exasperated letters and transatlantic phone calls were met with silence. The US copies of issue 3 had to be posted to subscribers directly from Scotland at greatly increased postage per copy. Our usual procedure, then as now, was to send them in bulk direct from the printer; they would then be posted out to individual subscribers from New York. This early hiccough was overcome when DePietro finally handed over subscriber details and Dana found Jennifer Goodrich, a writer friend in Hastings-on-Hudson, who offered to take on the role stateside from issue 4. Jennifer remains involved as an American Assistant Editor with the Horse to this day. She is a highly thoughtful, considered and literary writer (see page 170) who deals in a light spirit with the American side of the journal and occasionally contributes essays and reviews.

* * *

The Horse gets into its stride—kickbacks against New Formalism

I have written in such detail about those early numbers of the magazine because beginnings are fascinating. Thereafter, the Horse settled into a reasonably regular appearance—with some exceptions—twice a year. It retained the basic cover design it had started out with, varied only by different colour cover cards, through to issue 14. In those earlier days I took no money from the magazine and did not feel compelled to publish it to a strict schedule. Contents built up naturally (except with the prose, which must always be commissioned), and the Arts Council were then more relaxed in their expectations.

With issues 4, 5 and later, the journal was getting into its stride and establishing itself as a presence in the UK (and in its more modest way, the US) poetry scene. I attempted an overview of its reception in my editorial for issue 4 (see page 65). It was beginning, too, to show its regulars: among the UK writers, William Neill, Wendy Cope, Kirkpatrick Dobie, Helena Nelson, Anne Stevenson, Philip Hobsbaum; among the US contributors, Timothy Murphy, David Mason, R. S. Gwynn and Dana Gioia.

The predominant note was still polemic, and there were numerous cross-references: David Mason, for example, reviewing and referring to Philip Hobsbaum and his book on metre and verse form; Philip writing a brief affectionate memoir of meeting the great Irish poet Patrick Kavanagh in Dublin for the first time; me, reviewing Kavanagh's *Selected Poems*.

I think it was Howard Sergeant, the once-renowned editor of the long defunct poetry journal *Outposts*, who called publishing a little poetry magazine 'self-education in public'. One can see from my own reviewing where my preoccupations and animus lay. Here I am on Kavanagh:

> He was a sort of poet becoming increasingly rare now that poetry is more and more validated by degree and award, and more of a career than a vocation. Not having been artificially complicated or suppressed by too much literary theory, nor having felt their individuality subsumed into the imposing airs of the University English departments, this sort is often opinionated, iconoclastic and thrawn. Never having written an essay towards getting a degree, passion for poetry has to sustain them. This means that their literary knowledge, while it may be incomplete, is usually intense: they only read what they enjoy, or feel they can learn from.

—*The Dark Horse* 4, p64.

By issue 5 there was the first sign of a kickback against various assumed allegiances in the journal. Sometimes American correspondents would annoy me by their subsuming Scotland into England, so there was always a fair degree of emphasis on the journal's Scottish provenance, if not its purview: we had always published poets from throughout the UK, Ireland and Europe. My issue 5 editorial noted as follows, a touch tetchily, about one such assumption:

> Some time ago an American poet wrote in a letter, after seeing this magazine, that he was interested to observe that New Formalism had 'reached' Scotland. I resisted the temptation to reply. Suffice it to say that Scottish poets (and English, Irish, and Welsh poets) have practised metre and rhyme, and used narrative, since at least the 14th century. Almost every established poet in Scotland has shown some formal capabil-

ity at some time. William Neill [...] published in his *Selected Poems* of 1994 an intriguing blank verse narrative in Scots, 'The Harnpan' ('The Skull'), taken from an old Gaelic tale. Neill's poem was written long before the New Formalists were heard of here.

As if to emphasise our editorial independence (and indeed ex-emplify the Dark-Horse-as-unknown-quantity element of the journal's title), the issue carried a markedly qualified review of *Rebel Angels: 25 Poets of the New Formalism*, edited by David Mason and Mark Jarman. This was the signature anthology of the movement. The reviewer was the English poet, critic, novelist and publisher John Lucas. His notice pointed out that the Americans had come to rhyme and metre, as it were, sec-ondhand, so they should not get above themselves. If they did, their learned elders in the UK—owners of the great tradition on which they were drawing—might have to slap them down.

Horse 5 also contained a fascinating piece by the poet and critic Laurence Lerner, which—unusually for prose—had come in unsolicited, about the changing reception over three decades for a poem of his written in the voice of a woman. Non-showily erudite, yet plain speaking and personal, it is a model for the type of essay I have always been delighted to publish:

> Twenty years ago I began to realise how much a new genera-tion of women disliked the poem. The sharpest shock came when I gave a poetry reading to one of the many sixth forms I used to go and read to. I said, as I often did, to the teacher who had invited me that I thought everyone would get more out of the occasion if they had read some of my poems be-forehand. He replied that they had read 'A Wish' and that the girls were very angry about it. When Philip Larkin received a letter from 'a girl in Ramsgate' telling him how disgusting his poems were, he responded 'Whoops. The only ones she cited very *very* mild. Thank God she's in Ramsgate.' Well, these girls weren't in Ramsgate, and Larkin's ironic detachment was out of my range, so I would have to read the poem—but how?

* * *

A Journal of Poetry and Opinion

The Dark Horse

Ian Hamilton | *In Conversation*

Dana Gioia | *Fire & Ice: Robert Frost*

Edwin Morgan | *A Burns Celebration*

William Jay Smith | *Cummings v. Ashbery*

Philip Hobsbaum | *The Irish Difference*

Poems:

Iain Crichton Smith, William Neill, Tom Disch,

X. J. Kennedy, Anthony Hecht, A. D. Hope

No. 3

$5.00   £3.00

The last issue of the magazine to go spineless into the world. The printer produced among the print run a hundred or so faulty but not entirely unusable copies, which he reprinted. I was able to use the extra copies as giveaways.

A Journal of Poetry and Opinion

The Dark Horse

R. S. Gwynn | *The Advocates of Poetry*
Dana Gioia | *Interviews Howard Moss*
Weldon Kees | *American Jazz*
James Aitchison | *On Edwin Morgan*
Philip Hobsbaum | *Meeting Patrick Kavanagh*

Poems:
Anne Stevenson, William Neill, Dick Davis,

X. J. Kennedy, Gail White, David Mason

No. 4

$5.00

WINTER 1996-1997

£3.00

Our first issue with a spine and with Arts Council support. It also marked the first of a short run of anecdotal memoirs by Philip Hobsbaum on various literary encounters and acquaintances. 'Kavanagh looked exactly like my idea', he wrote, 'of an Irish hill-farmer: pot-bellied, bewhiskered, wearing a suit of stout tweeds and a battered trilby hat. The only incongruous touch was a pair of rather learned-looking spectacles'. Oxbridge academe meeting the heaven-taught ploughman.

May 31, 1995

Dear Mr. Cambridge,

I was very interested in The Dark Horse, first issue, and very heartily endorse the programme that it inaugurates — pleased as much by its flexibility as by its firmness.

To put my hand where my mouth is, I enclose a subscription and also four poems. Should these, or any of them, meet with your approval, I do not look for payment.

I'm very glad that Dana Gioia let me into the ground floor of this enterprise. If it runs into trouble, count on me to help out.

Yours sincerely,

Donald Davie.

This kindly letter, from Donald Davie, belied his reputation for fierceness. Some time after the publication of issue 1, I sent him a copy. In issue 3 we published his fine late poem, 'The Lost Bride', which begins:

'Versify it, Donald,'
I hear one of them say;
'Put it in rhyme, if I'm
To give it the time of day!'

And level-headed you
See the force of that:
'Unable to join the dance,
Sit still and sit it out.'

Dear vanished one, alive
As I have to imagine, your
Booted foot beats out: 'Not
Up to it any more.'

Editorial

To begin with an apology and a welcome: the first to our American readers who experienced difficulties obtaining issue 3, which was due to circumstances beyond our control; and the second to our new U.S. Assistant Editor, Jennifer Goodrich. Jennifer is primarily a writer of fiction, and has already brought an informed and intelligent eye to the magazine, as well as a new efficiency and enthusiasm.

With issue 4, it is appropriate to note that the Horse hasn't gone entirely unremarked. James Keery, in a substantial notice in *Poetry Review*, apparently had difficulty deciding whether he approved of the magazine or not. "You can see *The Dark Horse* coming a long way off," he wrote, whether in a tone of trepidation or weariness is unclear. "Again," he continued, "the poetry is *comparatively* fine [my italics], but it's a pleasure to turn to the sympathetic figure of Kirkpatrick Dobie, 'a solid citizen of Dumfries....' It's uncertain why "comparatively fine" poetry and Mr. Dobie's sympathetic figure, profiled in issue 1, are placed on different sides of that "but" — yet let it pass. Mr Keery's critical acumen, however, plummets in my eyes when he compares the magazine to its detriment with those which feature 'language' poets, a fall reinforced when reading the quotes of poetry he likes in other magazines, in the same review. Still, one is grateful for the attention.

Other reviewers have been less hesitant. "One of the best of the new poetry magazines," wrote the reviewer in OUP's *Critical Survey*, "to be found in the UK."

The responses of other editors have been interesting. Tim Kendall, an editor of the new Oxford-based magazine *Thumbscrew*, which aims for critical acerbity, complained after issue 2 that the Horse had not published any excellent poetry yet. I disagreed with him of course, but also made the obvious rejoinder about his — rather frail — glass house. "Some magazines," wrote poet-editor Brian Merrikin Hill in *Pennine Platform*, "begin tentatively like kittens learning to walk, but [*The Dark Horse*] springs Minerva-like into full maturity...." Hill is a forthright and sometimes trenchant critic. And the young editor of a new magazine in England writes that he considers *The Dark Horse* "clearly superior" to *Poetry Review*. The latter, for all its flashy handsomeness, has the same problem as any other poetry magazine: obtaining quality work. That may not be the same as fashionable work, or work by writers who have just won awards, or by writers who are hip on account of precocity.

If *Poetry Review* is not markedly better than other poetry magazines with smaller budgets, this simply shows that large resources don't necessarily pave a road to Parnassus. That said, *The Dark Horse* is put together with a combination of what can seem foolhardiness and dogged optimism, with a state-of-the-art — in 1988 — computer. We need more subscribers urgently. We are not above asking for benefactors.

To finish with a note on the tribulations of editing. During the summer, another editor complained to me that he sometimes received truly awful submissions accompanied by alluring photographs of their glamorous authors. Alas, no such submissions turn up in my mail — which may explain what I fondly hope is the high standard of work in this issue.

My editorial overview in issue 4 of the Horse's reception, at least up till that issue. The editor in the last paragraph was Bill Baer of *The Formalist*, a distinguished poetry journal out of Indiana. I spent a pleasant afternoon with Bill sometime around 1996 at Burns' Cottage in Alloway. I think I can guarantee that his editorial judgements were wholly unswayed by the circumstances mentioned.

A Journal of Poetry and Opinion

The Dark Horse

John Lucas | *On America's Rebel Angels*
Dana Gioia | *Charles Causley at Eighty*
Laurence Lerner | *The History of a Poem*
Edwin Morgan | *Scotland's Cornucopia*
Peter Dale | *The State of Modernism*

Poems:

John Haines, Andrew Hudgins, Ted Kooser,

Gabriella Mirollo, Tom Pow, Kirkpatrick Dobie

No. 5

$5.00   SUMMER 1997   £3.00

Issue 5 marked the beginning of a reaction against New Formalism. The interview was with Edwin Morgan. Surprisingly, perhaps, for a lifelong literary academic as well as a poet he was distrustful of Creative Writing as a discipline in the universities. 'What will [work produced on such courses] really be like? Will it have a strong pith of creative vigour or will that be made bland in some way by being homogenized just according to certain canons of how to produce something that the public will pick up and enjoy buying and reading?'

The Horse relocates—a famous address—Iain Crichton Smith—Morgan's take on Hughes' Birthday Letters

In August 1997 the caravan I had lived in for twenty years had been dismantled and sold for scrap. The spot where the magazine had been founded was unwalled air. I had moved on 31st August to Brownsbank Cottage near Biggar in Lanarkshire as poet in residence in Hugh MacDiarmid's former home. Issues 6 and 7, between autumn 1997 and early winter 1998/1999, were published from that distinguished address.

MacDiarmid, naturally enough, featured in the editorial of issue 6. 'I write this', I typed, surrounded by paintings of the great man all round the walls, 'under 14 portraits of Hugh MacDiarmid...' I only noticed later the comic unintentional ambiguity in that 'under': the sense of being almost buried by the poetic lineage was strong.

The issue's interview was with the major Scottish poet Iain Crichton Smith, actually in MacDiarmid's cottage (Iain sat in the great man's leather armchair). As a non-Scots-speaking Gael, Iain was refreshingly free of any expectation he should write in Scots—an expectation I was keenly aware of when living at Brownsbank. (It was not that I hadn't written in that tongue: I simply felt any such pressure as artistically compromising and, in a way, falsifying the natural impulse by which such things happened.)

The issue also carried a lengthy piece on MacDiarmid criticism by James Robertson, the first holder of the Fellowship I then occupied. James was a rather more dedicated MacDiarmid fan than I ever was—though I hugely admired the early lyrics, 'A Drunk Man Looks at the Thistle', and some of the later poems. All the politicking and opinionating and attitudinising, however, I was happy to leave to one side.

In a spirit of MacDiarmidean contrariness (which the publication had had since its inaugural number: I think that MacDiarmid would have hated the journal) issue 6 also continued a feature begun in our second issue.

This was to quote 'memorable' or otherwise remarkable examples of hyperbolic criticism or blurbs. The one featured, from a review of a Christopher Rick's edition of T. S. Eliot poems was, ironically, from *Thumbscrew*. The Horse's almost exact contemporary, the English journal *Thumbscrew* prided itself on its combative critical stance. It appeared to have modelled its tone on Ian Hamilton's *The Review*. I had had a few relatively good-natured run-ins with its editor, Tim Kendall, in its early days. I particularly enjoyed rebutting, in considerable detail, his assertions on the Horse's shortcomings in his casual handwritten letters (See page 74).

(See page 74).

* * *

A good deal had changed by the appearance of the following issue, number 7, around a year later. Iain Crichton Smith was dead, quite suddenly, from complications of cancer of the oesophagus. I had heard, by radio in Brownsbank, news of Ted Hughes' unexpected death on October 28th 1998. The Horse was about to run an unimpressed notice of the *Birthday Letters* by Edwin Morgan. It was one of the few reviews of that book by an equally gifted contemporary. Eddie asked that I insert a note indicating that the review had been written before the news of Hughes' demise. (Most people had not known that he was ill.) Near the opening of his review, after an unexpected—from such a relentless experimenter—'Yes, but is it art?', Morgan went on:

> I was reminded of D. H. Lawrence's remark: 'Art itself doesn't interest me, only the spirit content.' *Birthday Letters* has plenty of spirit content, but it gives little pleasure to the ear, it has a very rough music if music it is at all. The well-made, pulsing rhythms of Hughes's early poetry (pre-*Crow*) have been replaced here by a very free, thudding, often prosaic style which relies too frequently on the forced punchiness of verbless sentences. In tabloid journalism the verbless sentence is used to imply urgency and immediacy and downrightness: both the journalists and their supposed readers don't have time for syntax. But those poems are the fruit of a quarter of a century's writing and reflection, so why the finger-stabbing?

We could have a boiled-down *Birthday Letters* using a selection of Hughes's non-sentence sentences:

> First sight.
> Your daddy.
> Never the same.
> Over in a flash.
> Everything in negative.
> My children.
> Or some of them.
> And your grin.
> The thrill of it.
> Hiding from it and making it up.
> Especially for me.
> String ends too short to be saved.
> A tower of the Muses.
> Easy prey.
> Hellish.
> Yaddo fall.
> Macabre debate.
> Too much Alpha.

Horse 7 also ran the first ever published critical essay, by Dana Gioia, on the poet Kay Ryan. Now famous, at least in the small world of poetry, Ryan was then almost entirely unknown. As accompaniment, we printed eight of her compressed, paradoxical, multi-layered poems.

The issue opened with two remarkable pieces by the Russian poet Katia Kapovich, now living in America. Her poems had an authority of tone that would have been remarkable in a native speaker, never mind someone using English as a second language. It gave these verses a strange, sonorous dignity. In 'A Prison for an Architect', about the incarceration of her father, she wrote of his sudden disappearance:

> The sun-stamped envelope of morning held no note.
> Black sparrows chirped and dove in white and blue.
> The exposed film of early snow developed
> false footprints, to make a lie seem true.

Visiting him in prison, she found that

> Aloof and gray, he would approach the bars,
> his eyes, without a wink, revealed new wrinkles
> around them, shunned my own, shunned human farce:
> shunned faces, things, hovering like two eagles.

It was around this time, at Brownsbank, that I'd had the derisory postcard from Philip Hobsbaum calling me 'a literary amateur'. A new biography of the Scottish poet Andrew Young had just appeared. Philip had some unexpected enthusiasms; Andrew Young, that Scottish master of metaphor and quirky, unexpected insight, was one. Knowing of Philip's interest—he had all Young's books—I phoned and asked if he'd like to review the biography. He was extraordinarily appreciative, perhaps feeling he'd been overly severe on me. When I quoted from memory Young's beautiful 'Passing the Graveyard' ('I see you did not try to save / the bouquet of white flowers I gave; / so fast they wither on your grave'), he affected astonishment: 'My word, not even my colleagues in Glasgow's English Department could quote that!'

I took this as less a compliment to my memory than an indication of Philip's surprise that literature could actually have an independent existence and be absorbed meaningfully outside a university. That said, I have seldom encountered a literary academic for whom poetry seemed so *viscerally* important.

This also held true for William Neill, whom I interviewed in that issue. The interview began:

GC: When I think of you in relation to Scottish Poetry I align you with people like MacDiarmid, Tom Scott, and so on—mavericks.

WN: Oh, I feel a great affinity with mavericks. After all, if people are mavericks they must be getting near some kind of originality. If they're not mavericks, they're in the swim. They've got all their pals telling them what it's best to do. Mavericks do their own thing, like Crabbe, John Clare, Blake: the great originals.

* * *

A winter in Glasgow—Douglas Dunn—Hughes at
Cambridge—An American rival

The Dark Horse 8 wasn't published until the late autumn of
1999. I had left Brownsbank in September after my two-year
stint and spent that winter on Glasgow's Southside, flat-shar-
ing with an actress landlady. The cover of the new issue had
changed its strapline: 'A journal of poetry and opinion' (Dana's
suggestion originally, perhaps riffing off Robert Bly's polemical
The Sixties magazine) became 'The Scottish-American Poetry
Magazine.' I had intended the 'Scottish-American' to ground
the journal geographically, so bypassing London as the presumed centre of literary power in the UK. I wanted to exempli-
fy the fact, established by ventures like Bloodaxe and Carcanet,
that literary publishing of real quality was equally possible outside the centre. Occasionally, however, US readers had a problem with this new strapline, taking it to mean that the journal
was only open to contributors who were 'Scottish-American'.

The issue had a lime-green card cover. It had also been
slightly redesigned, with increased leading (line spacing) on
the prose and more white space around the text blocks. Earlier
that summer I had been exposed to design elements by the
remarkable house designer for Luath Press in Edinburgh, Tom
Bee, when Luath had published my second book, *'Nothing But
Heather!': Scottish Nature in Poems, Photographs and Prose*,
written when I was at Brownsbank cottage.

A major change was that the journal now had an email
address, though it would be some time before it developed
anything as remarkable as a real web presence. This change
represented the beginning of a major paradigm shift around
then, not just for the journal but for the world at large, from a
culture of post and traditional mail to online communication.
Thereafter, accepted prose or poems could be emailed, thus
saving my having to re-key everything.

Among the issue's highlights was an interview with the
Scottish poet Douglas Dunn. Late that summer, on a day of

astonishing sunlit beauty premonitory of autumn, I had travelled to his little Fife village to meet him. Dunn is, at the time of writing, Scotland's pre-eminent senior poet, whose work is notable for its considered humaneness, command of form, and a typically Scottish sympathy for the under-dog. He is a major figure whom the Horse has been able to call on for contributions since.

Another highlight was Hobsbaum's memories of an older era. 'Ted Hughes at Cambridge' was an anecdotal account of his encounters, when both were students, with this imposing figure. Not that Philip thought him so, exactly. His piece contained a note of denigration and an obsessive and unflattering fixation with elements of Hughes's personal appearance. I either didn't pick up on this or I overlooked it for the sake of having such a unique article in the journal. Philip was sensitive to anything he felt 'uncouth'. (He once reproved me for including, in a mining poem about my paternal grandfather, a memory of the ammoniac reek when my grandfather urinated into a chamber pot he kept under the bed.) However partial, though, his Hughes memoir offered a fascinating glimpse into a certain period in literary history. No one else involved with the magazine could have written it. Elaine Feinstein not long after quoted from it in her 2001 biography of Hughes.

It was around this time there was a dispute over the journal's name. The American poet Diane Thiel, whom I'd recently met, emailed me to ask if I knew that there was going to be an American *Dark Horse*, published out of a university? It was to be titled the *Dark Horse Literary Review*. She forwarded the editor's contact details, and I got in touch with her, requesting that she change the name—there already *was* an American *Dark Horse*, I said, and a second would not only cause confusion but profit unwarrantedly from the high reputation of the current Horse.

She replied that she had searched online when considering her magazine's title and, as we had no internet presence, hadn't been aware of us. She believed in a pluralist culture of magazines. There were many Dark Horses she said: she had no intention of changing her journal's name.

I couldn't see what, based in Scotland, I could do about a similarly-named American rival. I contacted Dana. For the first time we came close to having a serious dispute. 'Your email to her is so accommodating that I'm surprised Scotland is an independent country,' he wrote, displaying an illuminating lack of knowledge as to Scotland's status within the UK. I replied frostily that this was happening in the States, which was not my country; I felt helpless. He said, 'Leave it with me. We'll generate a Cease and Desist letter and have it sent to the Dean of the University. Such people are notoriously sensitive to any hint of institutional scandal.'

Working with a lawyer, he had a case drawn up for the preeminence of *The Dark Horse* and its existing claim on the name. The documents were duly sent. Less than a week later, the other journal changed its title.

* * *

20 November, 1995

Gerry Cambridge
19 Cunninghamhead Estate
By Kilmarnock, Ayrshire
Scotland KA3 2PY
Tel: 01294 850348

Dear Tim Kendall:

Thanks for the copy of Thumbscrew No. 3, and for the response to The Dark Horse, issue 2. I've just dipped into Thumbscrew, which looks lively and interesting. The Simic feature in particular looks great fun, and I'm glad to see the introduction of contributor's notes.

You'd be daft to class TDH as a dyed-in-the-wool formalist magazine. The editorial in issue 1 should have established that. What it does have is an overt concern for craft, for the notion of poetry as a making. 'Twas fun to see you bringing in Eliot. What about his introduction to the Faber selection of Kipling's verse? He states there, if my memory serves, that no great poet has ever been less than a master craftsman (or craftswoman). And of course one would have to have earmuffs on not to hear the music of Eliot's work. You may even be surprised to hear that I like Whitman, Jeffers, Ginsberg and Ferlinghetti! My animus is really against prose passing itself off as verse, free or otherwise. In my own practice as a poet, I have written both free and formal verse. But to me free verse is harder to write. Most practitioners regard it as easier, hence the flood of dull free verse printed almost everywhere.

Eliot is quite likely to be a great poet, but all this talk about who is "the greatest" is a bit boring, don't you think? Poets aren't boxers. Craft, or lack of it, is rather more open to examination than are the more subjective matters related to "assessing" poetry. (I can't be mithered with all this type of talk, by the way.) Eliot disliked Hardy's verse, to all accounts. Is Eliot 'greater' than Hardy, and who is going to say this? The University, or the common reader? Personally, I think Edward Thomas, in a number of his poems, is a 'great' poet, but I'm perfectly aware of the subjectivity of the statement.

Berryman doesn't surely need anything "doing" about him. He was a formal master -- look at his sonnets. His homage to the first lady of U.S. verse is surely one of the finest recent long poems from that side of the Atlantic, despite its loud echoes of Hopkins. His dream puffs may be a bit slacker and more shambling, but by god he earned it. And they read terrifically.

Take all this in good spirit. You have some impressive names in Thumbscrew, and I wish the magazine well. I'll be happy to exchange ads, and will make up one in a rectangular format for TDH for your next issue. I assume you can reduce it to fit, but if not let me know. TDH is printed from disk. I can make you up an ad. here if you don't need the font of your letterhead duplicated precisely, and provided you supply me with relevant details (of course). Otherwise, you'd have to send me the letterhead as a 'Tiff' or 'Pict' graphic, which I could import into the document, and on a Macintosh formatted disk. On second thoughts, don't bother with that. Just send me a large (say, x2 that you went below it. I'll do the rest. I'd need it by mid-March, but the sooner I have it the better.

I look forward to reading the rest of Thumbscrew. I hope that you disagree wildly with much of The Dark Horse, remembering what Blake said about disagreement.

All good wishes

Gerry Cambridge
Gerry Cambridge

P.S. - if you'd like to put your objections into slightly more organised form. I'm considering introducing a letters page, from #5 onwards.

One of my—doubtless very annoying—letters to Tim Kendall, editor of *Thumbscrew*, where I make responses to things he may not actually have said. As I recall, I cultivated a certain brisk persona in these letters. *Thumbscrew* in its critical acerbity was certainly one of the most interesting little magazines at the end of the millennium.

━━━ *A Journal of Poetry and Opinion* ━━━

The Dark Horse

Mario Relich | *The Poetry of A. C. Jacobs*
Anne Stevenson | *Elizabeth Bishop's Animals*
Timothy Murphy | *Meeting Robert Penn Warren*
Iain Crichton Smith | *In Conversation*
James Robertson | *MacDiarmid's Criticism*

Poems:
Edwin Morgan, Angus Martin, Gail White,
Jared Carter, Iain Crichton Smith, X. J. Kennedy

No. 6

$5.00   £3.00

SPRING 1998

The first issue produced at Brownsbank, Hugh MacDiarmid's former home. It contains Timothy Murphy's brief, pithy account of encountering his teacher at Yale, Robert Penn Warren. (See the leaflet on p93.) Warren's brutal, retributive 'The Ballad of Billie Potts' delighted me when I first read it in Richard Ellmann's *The New Oxford Book of American Verse* (1976). The poem may have been based on a true story from Illinois and I often wondered if it had influenced R. S. Thomas's fine narrative poem 'The Minister'.

A Journal of Poetry and Opinion

The Dark Horse

Kathleen Raine	*Russell's Quintilius*
Edwin Morgan	*The Birthday Letters*
Philip Hobsbaum	*The Green Man*
William Neill	*Mavericks, Satire, Scotland*
Helena Nelson	*The Muse Strikes Back?*

Poems:

Kay Ryan Special Feature, Dana Gioia, David Mason,

Kirkpatrick Dobie, Katia Kapovich, Rhina P. Espaillat

+ WELDON KEES'S LAST UNPUBLISHED POEM

$5.00

No. 7
WINTER 1998-99

£3.00

I had an occasional correspondence with Kathleen Raine in the 1990s, and so was able to call on her as a reviewer. This issue marked her only appearance in the Horse, with a characteristically deft and sophisticated review of Peter Russell's versions of the apocryphal Quintilius, a Latin poet of the early fifth century. The issue also printed the first ever critical consideration of Kay Ryan's poems, by Dana Gioia.

The Scottish-American Poetry Magazine

Philip Hobsbaum | *Ted Hughes at Cambridge*

Douglas Dunn | *In Conversation*

Dana Gioia | *On James Fenton*

Alasdair D. F. Macrae | *Remembering Iain Crichton Smith*

Mario Relich | *Conn and Stolen Light*

Poems:

Anne Stevenson, Edwin Morgan, Patty Scholten,

Michael Lind, R. S. Gwynn, Diane Thiel, Douglas Dunn

$5.00

No. 8

AUTUMN 1999

£3.00

A highlight of this issue for me was sonnets by Patty Scholten in versions by James Brockway, the renowned translator from the Dutch. A quirky, enthusiastic, learned and completely singular character, Brockway wrote letters part-handwritten, part-typed, which always delighted me.

The Horse Gets Into

its Stride:

1999–2005

quite a while at the poem in the issue. Squinting sideways, I saw it was by Richard Wilbur.

'Any good?' I said.

'Better than usual.'

'I've just come from a conference in Pennsylvania where there was a discussion about that particular poet.'

'Oh?'

'It was all about—the conference—using metre and rhyme as a way to bring a popular audience back to poetry.'

'I've known quite a few poets, including at least one famous enough for you to have heard of him.'

'Really?' Now I was intrigued. 'Who?'

'His name was Robert Lowell.'

'Robert Lowell!'

'Yes. I was a close friend. I used to be called when there was a danger he might need hospitalisation during one of his manic episodes.'

'That's some coincidence,' I said. 'I know his biographer, Ian Hamilton.'

'Yes, he came to see me several times when he was writing that book.'

'Here's another coincidence. In that rucksack'—I nodded to it on the rack opposite overhead—'I've a copy of issue 3 of the magazine I edit, *The Dark Horse*, with a long interview with Ian Hamilton, some of which talks about biography. You can have it, if you'd like, when we get off the train.'

We drew into Penn Station in New York, where I was met by Gabriella and said goodbye to the man I'd encountered, after first rummaging around for a spare copy of issue 3 in my rucksack on the concourse. 'I'm sorry—what was your name?'

'Blair Clark. You'll find me in the index of the Hamilton book.'

When I got back to Scotland, I looked him up in my copy of the Lowell biography. There he was, with numerous entries. Unprompted, he subscribed to the magazine. He died the following year, on June 6, 2000.

* * *

Two of the poets I met at the West Chester conference were Richard Wilbur and Anthony Hecht. On one occasion I found myself behind Wilbur, and in front of Hecht, in a queue for dessert. Turning back to Hecht I said, 'I've just realised I'm standing between two of the greatest American poets of the 20th century!'

'Well,' Hecht shot back, 'you're standing behind *one* of them.' He always deferred to Wilbur in the matter of literary quality.

Wilbur was a tall gentlemanly presence who reminded me, unexpectedly, of a Scottish hill farmer. I wrote to Eddie Morgan later about my surprise at this, considering the formal elegance of Wilbur's work, and toying briefly with the idea of a physiological basis for poetry. I think by that measure we both expected a small, dapper, immaculately turned out man with a bow tie and perhaps a monocle.

If Wilbur was outdoorish, even hearty (as many of his poems, read truly, would indicate), Hecht was a short man with a walking stick who manoeuvred around the conference with slow deliberation as if it took some effort to keep himself assembled. He seemed to carry his own personal cloud of gloom wherever he went. I knew something of his grievous personal history as a young Jewish-American soldier present at the liberation of Flossenburg, an annexe of Buchenwald in 1945. An accomplished linguist, he was asked to translate some of the survivors' accounts, experiences which affected him for years and watermark to some degree all his poetry. I found I was, uncharacteristically, more or less unable to strike up any proper or extended conversation with him. It would have been like talking with an Old Testament prophet.

One year he was giving a special lecture at West Chester. I don't remember the topic, only that the song from *Love's Labours Lost*, containing the lines 'Then nightly sings the staring owl / Tu-whit, tu-whoo, a merry note' came up for discussion. Some devilment took hold of me. I was sitting with the New York poet Kate Light. We had both been surprised by the formality of Professor Hecht's approach—he had begun by *reading out* from a typed lecture. I put up my hand. Professor Hecht gestured to me to speak. I was about to commit the sort of smart-arse-ish *faux pas* that, as I know from my own experience, teachers may find difficult, a compound of attention-seeking and show-offery.

'Professor Hecht,' I said, 'do you think it probable that Shakespeare didn't realise that his rendition of the Tawny Owl, *Strix aluco*, which is the commonest owl in Britain, would in fact have been a compound of two of the bird's calls together, the 'whoo' being part of the male's territorial call, the 'tu-whit' the female's response, often rendered as 'kee-wick!, kee-wick!'?

I mimicked the latter and, for good measure, like the boy of Winander in Wordsworth's 'The Prelude', interlaced my fingers and, blowing into them, hooted sonorously like a tawny owl. The notes quavered in the silence through the air-conditioned room.

There was a few seconds' pause. Professor Hecht gathered himself and put out a hand for support on a nearby table. After a further interval he said, 'I don't think Shakespeare would have been thinking so naturalistically', or words to that effect.

When the seminar finished and we stood about outside the room chatting, Timothy Murphy said, chuckling, 'I'll bet Tony Hecht has never had *that* happen in a lecture before!'

The incident, though, had a positive outcome. Back in Scotland, I wrote to Professor Hecht and further discussed naturalism in poetry. This led to an intermittent, rather formal correspondence (See page 91). On one occasion I addressed him as 'Dear Anthony'; back came his response, with its habitual 'Dear Mr Cambridge'.

* * *

A first double—cliques & conferences—the moose in the
classroom—death of an old poet

When the next issue of *The Dark Horse*, 9/10, was published, just in time for the 2000 conference, it showed the influence of my visit to the US the previous summer. It was also, in an attempt to catch up on its publishing schedule, a genuine double—at 144 pages it was exactly twice that of our then standard pagination. Handsome in a purple-mauve card cover, it had a four-page editorial which attempted an overview of the first ten issues, the first five years. The contents opened with one of the wittiest and most amusing pieces the journal has ever run, Mark Halliday's 'The Moose in Class', about his experience trying to teach a class of 11th graders (sixteen and seventeen year-olds) Elizabeth Bishop's long poem 'The Moose' on the last day before the Christmas holidays. It conveyed, in the lightest way, the difficulty of communicating, even with receptive students, a love for poetry:

> So I thought, *let us calmly inhale a great poem from the Norton and this room of goofy noise will become a place of meaning. Let it be something that will not sound ancient in the students' ears, let it not feel Hawthorney and mossy and Back-Then-ish* ... I flipped to the end of the Norton and upon 'The Moose' did my eye fall. Elizabeth Bishop: good poet, good enough so that 11th graders ought to know about her. Maybe? What must an 11th-grader definitely learn about poetry since 1945? Definitely? Moose? Young people are interested in animals, aren't they? My five-year-old son would want to hear any story about a moose; yes, but these students were sixteen and seventeen. Why could I not think of a sexy poem? In the Norton? Minutes were passing.
>
> Loudly and as-if-confidently I announced 'The Moose'. Because—didn't I admire this poem a lot in 1979? I believe I did. And isn't it about society vs. Nature? And isn't that a very big deal in American literature and isn't that what I am teaching?
>
> Bravely then did I begin reading 'The Moose' aloud [...] 'The Moose' emerged in its opening stanzas as something SO calm, so awfully calm as to be irredeemably grownup and descrip-

tive and dating from Back Then. 'The Moose' was sounding unsexy to an incredible degree. The stanzas resounded drily in the silence which I had imposed upon the room by exertion of glaring authority, and within seconds I felt hatred for Elizabeth Bishop. Obviously she had not written 'The Moose' with my class in mind and I felt this was terribly selfish of her. Great poet? Where was the sexy intensity? Bishop showed no awareness that this was the Friday before Christmas vacation.

With a low-humming cramping pain of regret in my abdominal region I saw three or four of the better students actually trying to get their heads into 'The Moose,' actually trying for my sake or poetry's sake or for the honor of the school to frown their way into what some dead lady (did he say she was a *bishop?*) had written supposedly about some moose except there wasn't any moose—not yet—there was just this old bus driving along some old cold highway...

This piece had come to me via Helena Nelson, who in 2005 would go on to found Happen*Stance* Press, now one of the UK's most respected small presses for poetry—all achieved without external funding of any kind. Helena is not only a fine poet but an acute and idiosyncratic critic and reader who has frequently contributed essays and poems to the journal. She was represented in the double issue by a typically interrogative piece reviewing two recent books about New Formalism, as well as an interview with Anne Stevenson—another of the magazine's frequent poet-critics. A gifted poet whose work often found a home in the Horse's pages, Stevenson was senior enough to be relatively fearless and had a pronounced sceptical take on contemporary poetry culture. From very early on, she had been a vocal and valued supporter of the magazine—another of those maverick and exhilaratingly opinionated spirits who I felt, to some degree, validated the existence of a journal such as ours.

I was very happy to have such estimable female critics willing to write for the magazine. Gender imbalance was beginning to be raised as a problem in regard to the Horse. I was pragmatic about this in those days: the magazine could not print what it did not receive, and few women writers suggested writing prose for us. I am now much more active in commissioning women critics—a point I will return to.

Our first double issue was lively, but its relative showcasing made it appear cliquish. R. S. Gwynn contributed an amusing essay, 'The Egregious Faults of X. J. Kennedy', admiring this poet in the guise of outraged disdain, as well as a series of parodies of Gioia, Kennedy, Timothy Murphy, Wendy Cope and Richard Wilbur, under the general title 'How Many Poets Does It Take To Change a Light Bulb'. But such parodies, like the Kennedy essay, relied on the reader having sufficient background knowledge and familiarity with the originals parodied to see the joke. Understandably, some readers were baffled.

No doubt to balance up this American bias, I had included a quirky and seeming-casual piece by Hamish Whyte, poet-editor of Mariscat Press, about a trip round Edwin Morgan's Glasgow haunts, and Professor Hobsbaum reviewing in high critical style and in the context of his historical literary knowledge three new poetry anthologies. I had once responded dubiously to a young critic who'd suggested I send him any books I thought 'deserved a kicking' with 'but *you* might not think they do.' Nonetheless, one still chooses a reviewer for a particular book hopeful that they will at least say what they think.

By the time a poet has reached a particular point of eminence or fame, however, honest disinterested reviewing is about the last thing they can expect—and, quite possibly, wish for. For examples in relatively recent literature of unhindered truth-telling one thinks of Iain Crichton Smith's 'The Gowden Lyric', an inspired takedown of Hugh MacDiarmid's verbose later poetry, or Dana Gioia's masterly, forensic summation 'The Successful Career of Robert Bly.' Where such pieces appear to be motivated by *ad hominem* dislike, they lose credibility. Pieces like the two just mentioned are exemplary, and doubtless unsettling to their subjects, through such disinterested engagement with the work.

The 'ordinary' reader has no idea of the difficulty of obtaining honest reviewing about living contemporary poets. Poet-reviewers function in a compromised poetry culture. I am often amused to see, on some social media thread or other, lengthy discussions of such quandaries presented as fresh revelations. The issues around critical independence (when one is a poet) also extend to editorial independence. In the double number's editorial I wrote this:

> There are three main ways of editing with integrity.
> The first is not to be reliant on the poetry world for income.
> The second is not to be a poet, and therefore not concerned, in terms of whom one offends in the poetry world, about the opinions of others regarding one's own poetry. For unless you are like Wendy Cope, say, and actually popular, your reputation, sales, and other opportunities are likely to come primarily from the poetry world.
> The third, if, sadly, you're both a poet and not financially independent, is to be half mad. That is to say, heedless of consequences—or constitutionally incapable of printing a poem unless you think it deserves it.
> Being a recluse can also be an advantage. In this way you avoid the distasteful business of having to reject work by, or review negatively, people whom you have met and liked.

By this double issue, Kirkpatrick Dobie had died. He was buried with his manual typewriter. Kirkie was a typewriter person—his letters to me were always typed on a prized manual. Once, he sent me an account of trying to come to grips with the alarming, lightning unpredictability of a new electric typewriter—swiftly, I think, discarded. He signed off:

```
Any suicide note I leave as a resuly [sic] of
this new purchase will be in longhand.
```

At his funeral event in Dumfries I recall whiskies with the poet Hugh McMillan and others in *The Hole in the Wa'*, a famed Dumfries hostelry, at 9.30am. The pub had the appearance of having been open all night. It was the passing of an era. That double issue of the Horse reprinted my obituary for Kirkie from the [Glasgow] *Herald* and included four new poems, all of them of value. Dobie can be like Hardy—a decided influence—

in that even his more modest pieces are of interest. Here is one from the issue:

Mrs Betty McGeorge

Betty, brought home from nursing home to die —
an old woman — still would cry
for home.
'It isn't home!' she'd say
her fingers plucking at the overlay.

'Sure! Sure it is! There is the tree
you planted. You can see
the top, and just beyond it's the first tee
at Nunfield.
Listen, and you can hear them at their game.'

And she would look and listen
keenly, but always came
that odd disturbing disavowal:
'It's like it, but it's not the same.'

As John Crowe Ransom often did, Dobie titles his poem with the subject's name. The piece is typical, technically, of his work, using rhyme as a binding device, but irregularly. With its paradoxical, otherworldly conclusion in the statement by 'an old woman' poised spookily on the edge of mortal existence it confirms what Ann Karkalas had written in her essay in our inaugural issue on this poet. His poems 'make the familiar seem strange,' she observed, 'but not at all as a deliberate shock-effect. The strangeness belongs to the world.'

* * *

```
                                    28.vii.01
                                    4256 Nebraska Avenue, NW
                                    Washington, DC 2--16
        Dear Mr. Cambridge

        I hope that well before this letter reaches you my remarks on
        Richard Wilbur, that I promised to send you, will have arrived.
        As I knew you had agreed with George Core at the Sewanee Review,
        I sent a copy of the same remarks to him; and I understand that
        both your journal and his will acknowledge the double publication.

    I'm deeply grateful to you for your wonderful pamphlet, The Praise
    of Swans, which I have read admiringly. And thank you also for
    the fine photograph of the owl, and for your thoughtful and in-
    formative observations about owls. It seems to me that beasts
    and fowl in Shakespeare are almost always employed emblematically
    or symbolically, as in "The Phoenix and the Turtle," but also in
    the Macbeth lines, "Night thickens and the crow/Makes wing to the
    rooky wood" and in the lines about the cock-crow at the start of
    Hamlet; there was much popular lore about the creatures that had
    little factuality or truth about it. Moreover, from medieval
    times there were conventional ways of representing the calls of
    certain birds, employed, for example, in the French madrigal
    "Le Chanson des Oiseaux" and in Lyly's lines (echoed by Eliot)
    "What bird so sings, yet so does wail?/Oh, 'tis the ravished
    nightingale./Jug, jug, jug. jug, tereu, she cries..." Clearly,
    no accurate imitation of the nightingale's song is intended.
    I have heard nightingales in Italy, and the remarkable thing
    about their call is that it is not composed of a string of
    notes that are repeated. Each bird-call is a unique melodic
    improvisation. The Vatican radio station uses a nightingale
    motif for its call signal; but it is obliged to repeat the
    same sequence of notes for indentification purposes.


        I look forward to reading your comments on my work whenever you
        may send them, and I can say, regarding my unwillingness to
        lecture on my own work,   that I think such self-comment is
        unseemly. I can point with pleasure to the merits of other
        poets, but don't care to do so with my own work.

        Please let Philip Hobsbaum know, if you are in touch with him,
        that I greatly respect the book he wrote on Robert Lowell, and
        am accordingly very pleased that he likes my poetry.

        With grateful good wishes,
```

This is Hecht's response to the first letter I wrote him after our owlish encounter in the US referred to on page 85. His letters were all characterised by their old world courtesy, decorum and thoughtfulness. The Horse was publishing an essay by him on Richard Wilbur's work, later reprinted by *The Sewanee Review*. My 'comments' on his work referred to was, in fact, a 12,000 word essay for Scribners' *American Writers* series. He was a poet that Philip Hobsbaum held in something approaching awe, and so the latter was delighted when I relayed to him the contents of the last paragraph of Hecht's letter.

The Scottish-American Poetry Magazine

The Dark Horse™

Mark Halliday	*The Moose in Class*
Carolyn Kizer	*Ruth Pitter Reclaimed*
Anne Stevenson	*On Hype, Plath, Reputations*
Timothy Murphy	*Prairie Farming and Poetry*
Helena Nelson	*New Formalism: a U.K. Response*
R. S. Gwynn	*X.J.K's Egregious Errors*
Angus Calder	*Mason's* Poetry of Life *Essays*
Philip Hobsbaum	*Three 20th Century Anthologies*

Poems:

Wendy Cope, Dana Gioia, Donald Justice,

Edwin Morgan, Patty Scholten, Diane Thiel, Angus Martin

$10.00   **9/10**   £6.00
SUMMER 2000

Launched in the US, this was one of the few issues in which I published a poem of my own. The poem was 'Madame Fi Fi's Farewell', the title piece of my third collection. This issue also published a stanza by the Scottish writer Des Dillon, 'Wilderness of a Leaf': 'The world's whatever size you want it to be—/ Claustrophobia in New York / Or a child's gaze wandering / The wilderness of a leaf.' Now I would probably ask him to make more of the title. The issue closed with Diane Thiel's beautiful, resonant poem 'Echolocations', about a 'dead' whale—the title poem of her first book.

The front and back of a four-page *Dark Horse* publicity leaflet, brought out after the first double issue. Ordering details and other information would have been on the inside.

Top: from left to right, June 2009, Mike Peich, master printer, Richard Wilbur, and Dana Gioia. Mike and Dana co-founded the West Chester Poetry Conference in 1995. Below: one of many remarkable characters at West Chester, the poet, musician and carpenter Wilmer Mills photographed at the conference in summer 2009.

Above: Kate Light, poet and professional violinist, photographed in Bryant Park, New York city, in June 2008. Kate's poetry was characterised by its deft, quicksilver following of the turns and divagations of her own thought; stylistically, her work is highly distinctive. She had no props for this photograph; I said, 'But you're a writer, you've got to have a pen and a notebook, at least!', and lent her mine.

Below, right: N. S. Thompson, poet, critic, translator, at the West Chester Poetry Conference in Pennsylvania in June 2008. He has contributed numerous poems, critical essays and reviews to the Horse since the late 1990s.

One of my favourite American poets. X. J. Kennedy at the West Chester Poetry Conference in Pennsylvania, June 2007. 'Kennedy's work', I wrote elsewhere, 'has, at times, a devil-may-care heedlessness, reflected in his poetry's [frequent] preoccupations with sexual peccadillos and a wide range of unusual characters—many of them outsiders.' The 'X' does not stand for Xavier or Xerxes; it is made up.

*Poetic characters—Angus Calder, Horatian—9/11 and
American poetry—a monetary dispute—scrawny
independence & the little magazine*

Issue 11 was the last number of the Horse published before
9/11. It opened with some remarkable versions of Horace,
updated to a contemporary register and set in modern-day
Edinburgh by Angus Calder. This English-born Scottish polymath had received an Eric Gregory Award as a young man,
then largely abandoned poetry before returning to it in his
later middle age. His Horace versions—reviewed in the issue
by Helena Nelson—are memorable mixes of high and low reg-
isters, slangy Scots street speech and latinate English. Their
Edinburgh settings, often in pubs, give them contemporary
savour and a comforting everydayness.

Angus was an alcoholic who kept unusual hours. He once
phoned me at 3.30am; when I lifted the phone, heart ham-
mering in anticipation of a family death, there was a slight
pause; then the voice on the other end of the line said coolly and confident of immediate discussion, 'Gerry, I've been
thinking a lot recently about metric in the early formal poems
of Robert Lowell.'

On one occasion during an extended conversation in
the flat in Glasgow I shared with an actress in the winter of
1999/2000, I asked her to talk to him while I went to the toilet. I knew that the conversation would be quite capable of
spinning out for hours, so I also went and lay down for a nap.
Half an hour later, my flatmate summoned me: Angus was
asking that I be put back on the line. When I resumed my part
in the conversation, he said, by way of an aside before continu-
ing on some literary topic or other, 'Ah Gerry, I see that you are
back from your perambulation of the world's largest toilet.'

Issue 11 also ran a reminiscence by Hobsbaum of Hugh Mac-
Diarmid which painted the latter as a homophobe in regard to
'aspersions', as they were then cast, about Edwin Muir's sex-
uality. In their revelations of MacDiarmid's attitude, these are
embarrassing to read now. (You could never tell, of course,
whether MacDiarmid was being serious.) The pagination of
the issue reached, for the first time, 80 pages.

[97]

By the appearance of issue 12/13, another double, in early 2002, the world had changed. There was a great sense, after the tragedy of 11 September 2001, of the US closing its borders. I had been to the West Chester Poetry Conference each June since 1999; I would not return, and in truth I didn't wish to, until 2007.

The American element of the journal after 9/11 continued, but with less intimacy than before. In retrospect, Horse-wise at least, this was a good thing: the magazine had been in danger latterly of seeming only the vessel for a clique of favoured writers. This shift would be buttressed when, in 2003, Dana Gioia took up the post of Chairman for the National Endowment for the Arts in Washington, DC. It was a governmental position which meant he had to stand down from any literary affiliations which might indicate partiality.

Number 12/13, with an almost fluorescent orange card cover, opened with an account in my editorial of an episode still sometimes referred to with amusement in the literature section of Creative Scotland—which was, at the time, the Scottish Arts Council.

In those days I cultivated an air of scrawny independence in relation to State funding. I would apply only grudgingly for assistance with the journal's costs. When the 'Grants to Magazines' panel awarded *The Dark Horse* an additional £1,360 a year, they also decreed it should be 'strictly ring-fenced' for paying writers. I refused the extra money. For one thing, I hadn't asked for it. For another, I wrote that 'the funding body was simply assuming my willingness to be its unpaid administrator.' I suggested that 'it supply extra funds for such administration or, ideally, administer such payments itself.'

It is to the funding body's credit that this attitude did not result in the Horse having its funding withdrawn. If anything, it established the journal as a venture that would only apply for monies it really needed.

Hobsbaum revisited—the Horse slows to a trot—
Peter Redgrove & Boris Slutsky

Issue 14 was, in large degree, a special number on Philip Hobsbaum at 70. Peter Porter and Peter Redgrove contributed poems dedicated to him. The poet-critic James McGonigal wrote a fascinating and slightly ambiguous account of experiencing Hobsbaum as a teacher both pugnacious and invigorating. Jay Parini contributed an essay making a case for Philip's poetry—'bracingly concrete, with a ferocious, no-nonsense weather of [its] own.' Of the poetry at its best, this is fair.

I also interviewed Philip for the issue; we got into an amusing exchange when he criticised Ian Hamilton, who had died on the 27 December 2001. Hamilton had reviewed Philip's first book, *The Place's Fault* (1964), three times: 'once under his own name, once under a pseudonym, and once anonymously—and each time negatively.' Despite that, Philip '[bore] him no ill will'. In the interview he made reference to Hamilton's Third at Oxford, at which I bristled and indicated that I thought academic qualifications entirely irrelevant to poets:

GC: The final chapter of your book, *Essentials of Literary Criticism*, quotes with approval extracts from essays by Leavis, G. Wilson Knight, and D. H. Lawrence, but implies that if students ever actually write like that they'll never pass an exam...

PH: Well, not quite...

GC: More or less, and that it can backfire badly. So, what does that say about genuine creativity as opposed to what is expected of one in academe?

PH: I see your subtext. This is all anti-academy! [Laughter.]

Issue 14 was also the final number which had a plain, coloured card cover printed with black text. I was becoming more interested in design and layout. From issue 15, all Horse covers would be printed full colour on white stock board. This infinitely increased design possibilities, though issues 15 to 17 were recognisably based on the house design since issue 1, except with another colour as well as black added. The white board also meant that reversed text—white on a background colour—was now economically viable.

* * *

I was becoming more interested in the magazine's inner typography too. After being set in New Century Schoolbook throughout its run, issues 12/13 and 14 had seen a switch to Times New Roman. For issues 15 to 18, I used Jan Tschichold's Sabon, a face I had encountered because it was the house typeface of my then publisher, Luath Press, which would shortly publish my third book, *Madame Fi Fi's Farewell and Other Poems*. While hardly perfect, the new Horse design was 'cleaner', with more generous—perhaps too generous—leading on the prose, and the poetry printed for emphasis in a larger point size. I had also, some time before, dropped such abominations as underlining the poet's name (already in bold capitals, non-letterspaced) at the head of each author's contribution.

These four numbers—15 to 18—were different for other reasons. Dana, in one of his rare communications following his appointment as NEA Chairman, referred (in an aside I found comic) to the 'languid trot' that the Horse's publishing schedule had slowed to. Issue 15 bears the date Summer 2003; Issue 18, Summer 2006: four issues in three years. The sporadic publication dates were for several reasons. One was that I was busy with other projects: the magazine was only a modest part of my freelancing activities, a substantial component of which was my own writing. Another was difficulties in my private life.

Nonetheless, the magazines, when they did appear, showed no lessening of standards. (See page 107). Different names began featuring on the covers; what I had, some time before, begun to consider the tedium of much New Formalist writing was quietly phased out. A surprise package had arrived in early 2003 when issue 15 was in preparation—a prose piece on MacDiarmid by Seamus Heaney, sent in apology for his having missed the Hobsbaum number to which, as a long time friend of the older man, he'd been invited to contribute. Philip also penned a personal memoir and critical overview on the remarkable Peter Redgrove, a 'scientist of the strange' often associated in style with Ted Hughes but in reality greatly different. Accompanying six visionary new poems in Redgrove's late 'stepped verse' style, Hobsbaum's piece had an affectionate, occasionally scabrous intimacy that only an old friend and admirer could get away with. Here he is, recalling his first meeting with this poet 51 years earlier in 1952:

> In those days, when he had hair, Redgrove bore a resemblance to Frankenstein's monster; only better dressed. He said in comfortably middle-class tones, 'Thank you, my foot is quite warm now', signalling that I had inadvertently placed my briefcase on his toes. Neil Morris read first, Yeats's 'Prayer for my Daughter'. Somebody—not me—volunteered to read 'The Exequy' by Henry King. The putative reader, whoever he was, fumbled to find the place in Herbert Grierson's anthology, *Metaphysical Lyrics and Poems*. Redgrove said, 'You will find 'The Exequy' on page 203'; and so he did.
>
> Who was this person, whose well-bred voice was at variance with his threatening appearance, and who appeared to know the page numbers of every poem in the English language?

Another piece from issue 15 was Angus Calder's 'Discovering Boris Slutsky'—the verb in the title to be taken literally. His piece did what little magazines are perfect for: introduce readers (and the journal's editor) to poets of real substance largely overlooked by the 'mainstream' poetry culture.

I found Slutsky's aesthetic of plainness fascinating. I have a fundamental disagreement with the idea, commonly put around now, that poetry to which one must return time and again to mine its full range of meanings is *indisputably* the pinnacle of the art, and that the clear and memorable expression of feelings whether complex or simple is somehow a lesser thing. Where does that leave, for instance, the Border Ballads? Here is Calder on Slutsky's attitude:

> With his working class provincial origins, Slutsky was deeply suspicious of the aristocratic tradition which Akhmatova embodied. He detested the idea, commonplace in Russia, that the poet was a transcendent being, as much as he did the bardic addiction to alcohol which often went along with it. His dedication to his craft was lifelong and complete, but he tried to write poetry 'as plain as porridge' and give expression to ordinary people. His verse is deliberately non-sensuous, eschewing metaphor and even epithets of colour. [...] Basically, Smith reports, 'translating Slutsky's poetry is not easy first and foremost because he says exactly what he means.'

As an example, he quoted one of Smith's translations. Here are the first two stanzas:

> Four copies is the size of my editions.
> The typewriter can barely make a fifth.
> Nevertheless my heart is always steady,
> I have no vanity to make it lift.
>
> And while some idiot is bleat-bleat bleating
> For a huge crowd that doesn't give a hoot,
> I'm trying to choose the three very best readers
> In my own most immediate neighbourhood.

* * *

Issue 15 was also marked by a controversy which saw the Horse's first contentious appearance in the pages of the *Times Literary Supplement*. I had written in the Horse's Editorial:

> The news that 300 unpublished poems by Hugh MacDiarmid have been unearthed among the poet's papers in the National Library of Scotland by the methodical researches of the man-of-letters John Manson was greeted with headlines in *The Herald*. They focused on MacDiarmid's view in one poem that the razing of London by bombs in 1940 might not be such a bad thing. (*The Sunday Times* quickly followed up with a piece by Angus Calder based on the same poem.) Leaving aside the irony, considering MacDiarmid's lifelong poverty, of the £250,000 paid by the library in 1990 for these papers, Robert Frost's comment on Robert Lowell—'Oh, Robert will say anything for the hell of it'—surely applies equally to MacDiarmid. Who cares, really, beyond a sort of gossipy controversy, what MacDiarmid thought of the London bombing, especially in such an average example of his verse? Among the 300 new pieces seem some remarkable not for their opinionating—which is easy—but for their insight into existence, which is not: *The Herald* and *The Sunday Times* would surely have been better focusing on those instead. Less likely to make headlines, and considerably harder to write about, but more significant in the long term.

James Campbell, writing in his 'NB' column in the *TLS*, noted that one of these poems, 'on the subject of the Blitz, describes London as a 'foul disease', and states that the poet would 'hardly care' if the city was devastated by Germans.' He went on to say, with an uncharacteristic vehemence perhaps stirred by the fact that he was based in London:

> Press comments that followed these revelations make the *Dark Horse* editorialist impatient. 'Who cares, really, beyond a sort of gossipy controversy, what MacDiarmid thought of the London bombing?' Who cares, indeed? Scarcely anyone among the Scottish literati seems to care that MacDiarmid

[103]

continues on page 108

The Scottish-American Poetry Magazine

The Dark Horse

Helena Nelson | *The Case of Muriel Stuart*
John Lucas | *On W. S. Graham's Letters*
X. J. Kennedy | *Douglas Dunn: A U.S. View*
Philip Hobsbaum | *The Informal MacDiarmid*
Dana Gioia | *On America's Unsung War Poet*
David Mason | *Wilbur's Constant Spirit*
Edwin Morgan | *Attila József: Major Poet*

Poems:

Kate Light, Dick Davis, Andrew Hudgins,
Daniel Hoffman, D. M. Black, Rhina P. Espaillat, Chryss Yost,
Frederick Morgan, James Brockway, Annemarie Austin

$5.00

11
SPRING 2001

£3.00

One of the advantages of a transatlantic journal: asking reviewers to review, as it were, transatlantically—hence X. J. Kennedy on Douglas Dunn. John Lucas's review of W. S. Graham interestingly devoted its opening to design matters, recounting an amusing dispute between Graham and Charles Menteith involving an ornament Faber had put between Graham's poem titles and the poems' beginnings. This issue also marked, with two pieces, the first appearance in the magazine of the New York poet and violinist Kate Light. A lively and entirely individual spirit, she died tragically young in April 2016. The issue had bulked up to 80pp from our then-standard 72.

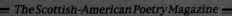
The Scottish-American Poetry Magazine

Carl Wilmore | *Robert Frost in 1916*
Anthony Hecht | *A Tribute to Richard Wilbur*
Anne Stevenson | *Poetry and the Planet*
John Lucas | *Poetry and Political Correctness*
Helena Nelson | *A Note on Eleanor Farjeon*
Dana Gioia | *U.S. Poetry and September 11*
Gerry Cambridge | *The Example of William Neill*
David Cameron | *Hope on Norman Cameron*

Poems:

Lynn Chandhok, Frank Dullaghan, G. F. Dutton, X. J. Kennedy,
Marcia Menter, Edwin Morgan, Catherine Tufariello, Gregory Woods

$10.00   **12/13**
WINTER 2001-2002   £6.00

Number 12/13 opened with Dana Gioia's 'All I Have Is a Voice', an article about having to do a poetry reading in Southern California on September 12, 2001, in the immediate aftermath of 9/11. I also printed a substantial section from Rab C. Wilson's memorable version of the *Ruba'iyat* into Scots. Here's 151:

> The mug thon workman drinks his tea frae
> Micht've been moulded frae the clay o kings.
> The bottle in that jakey's haun
> Could've been blawn frae the dust o some lost princess.

The Scottish-American Poetry Magazine

The Dark Horse

14
$5.00   SUMMER 2002   £3.00

The Philip Hobsbaum special issue. It also featured Dana Gioia's essay about the poetry of one of 'the major American men of letters of the past half-century', Frederick Morgan, the distinguished editor and founder of *The Hudson Review*. Gioia ruminates fascinatingly on the reasons for Morgan's relative, and by Gioia's lights unjust, neglect as a poet.

Opposite: Our first major cover redesign since issue 1, and a postcard from Dana responding to the change. The 'three American voices' headlined on the front cover were, as Dana mentions, X. J. Kennedy, B. H. Fairchild—whose magnificent poem 'Body and Soul', about baseball, the reviewer picked out for special praise—and Kate Light.

THE SCOTTISH-AMERICAN POETRY MAGAZINE

The Dark Horse ™

Seamus Heaney *MacDiarmid's Earthy Sublime*
Philip Hobsbaum *Fifty Years of Peter Redgrove*
Angus Calder *Discovering Boris Slutsky*
John Lucas *The Scottish Dream Staters*
Kathleen McDermott *On Three American Voices*
N.S. Thompson *Philip Hoy in Interview*
Mario Relich *On G. F. Dutton*
Jennifer Reeser *A Note on Sara Teasdale*
James Aitchison *Obscurity in Poetry*

Poems

Douglas Dunn, Edwin Morgan, Peter Redgrove, Diane Thiel,
Gael Turnbull, Jon Mooallem, Jon Stallworthy, Mike Stocks

$5.00

15

£3.00

SUMMER 2003

Office of the Chairman

Dear Gerry,   August 11, 2003

   The new issue of The Dark Horse looks fantastic!
Just my luck. As soon as I leave the editorial board
of the journal, you make it look classy. You now
seem positively establishmentarian. I particularly like
the way you made all of the improvements without losing
any of the particular character of the magazine--perfect
evolution rather than a mere change. I've been so busy
that every time I pick up the journal, the phone rings,
but I like the idea of interviewing Hoy the Interviewer.
And I am delighted to see Kennedy, Fairchild, and Light
reviewed. I was disappointed in Stallworthy's poem because
his best poems are just terrific. Moallem and Thiel were
both funny, and Morgan very fine.

   My life is all work--every day and every night--but
things are getting done. The Scottish Arts Council visited
me last month, and I put in a good word for you, not that
it seemed to be needed. They admire you.

worshipped Lenin, admired Stalin as a superman, supported the suppression of the Hungarian uprising, wrote a 'Plea for a Scottish Fascism', and never recanted lines such as 'What maitters 't wha we kill / To lessen that foulest murder that deprives / Maist men o' real lives'. Who could care less that he would have happily seen London and Londoners obliterated by the Nazis?

Predictably, this led to a flurry of letters in a subsequent issue, with the MacDiarmid scholar, John Manson, discoverer of the letters, and the Ayrshire poet, Sam Gilliland, piling in. The paper published my response too:

LETTERS TO THE EDITOR

MacDiarmid and the Blitz

Sir, – It seems to me that most of the Scottish literati are not so easily duped as to pay more than cursory attention to Hugh MacDiarmid in his self-elected role as pulpiteer and political prophet. Ultimately, it is the best of his poetry which is important, not his political opinions. My impatience, as the "*Dark Horse* editorialist" quoted in your columns (NB, July 18), is with those who not only manage to take such attention-seeking opinions of MacDiarmid seriously, but indeed give them breathing space. As is plain, however, from the column inches recently prompted by MacDiarmid's mediocre verses about the Blitz, what Douglas Dunn had called this poet's "talent for posthumous controversy" not only lives on, but flourishes.

GERRY CAMBRIDGE

* * *

A takedown—meeting G. F. Dutton, poet-scientist

Issue 16 provided one of the few occasions when I felt inclined to bring Professor Hobsbaum, like some massive muscly gladiator, out into the arena. The American poet and critic Joseph Salemi had sent me an essay similar to other pieces from around that time; his was called 'Why Poetry is Dying'. The article was not strong enough to publish as a standalone, but I wrote to Salemi and offered to print it on condition that I also run a response to his contentions from Professor Hobsbaum. Here is Philip limbering up for what would be more or less a point-for-point rebuttal:

> Literary criticism is a profession. Plenty of people aspire to be critics, but they do not always recognize what that activity entails. To be a critic, one needs to have read a very great deal. The difficulty lies in convincing those with critical aspirations how little they know.

I disagreed, of course, with the idea that criticism is only for professionals. Philip probably would have too, but when in demolition mode he adopted this attitude: the gladiator put on his helmet and took up his shield of professional pride.

He would certainly have taken umbrage at an opinion expressed in an interview in our following issue, number 17, but by then he was dead, after various problems with his diabetes which eventually led to the amputation of a foot. (This had, however, given him the opportunity to joke blackly about his new piratical status.)

I had travelled to Perth in Autumn 2004 to interview the poet-scientist, G. F. Dutton. He lived with his wife in a simple wooden house in the Perthshire hills surrounded by trees and a 'marginal' garden—basically, one located on a hillside— which he had planted 50 years earlier. In the interview Dutton described Leavis, one of Hobsbaum's heroes, as:

[a] hopelessly subjective man with good objective criteria, which he met in many cases; but Leavis had no sense of the music of language; none whatever. The early poems of Edith Sitwell are good early poems; they're musical; he had no idea about them at all, banished the whole lot with his usual rudeness. Criticism is very helpful if it goes into the work and enlightens; it's important also to give some encouragement, I think. The non-professional reader in a sense is more helpful, if he has a good mind; a professional critic is more likely to be misled by the work of being a critic: as in, how can I show this fellow he's useless? Show the bad points, yes, but only if showing the good points as well. It's easy to show the bad points, and one gets so much kudos for doing so: tough guy, he certainly showed them something, made them think: *that's the stuff to gie the bugger, eh, eh? Ah kent his faither!* * There's naethin there! Ah kent his faither, an he wis nae bluidy use [laughter]!

*'Ah kent his faither' is a Scottish phrase of denigration, characteristically applied to someone who is judged to have got 'above themselves'; roughly it translates as 'I knew his father [so he himself can't be that great]'.

Dutton was then 81. (See facing page.) He had been a biochemist of near-Nobel prizewinning level—'more than one Nobel Prizewinner has broken bread at this table,' he said when I visited to interview him.

As a young, groundbreaking researcher he had turned down far more lucrative offers from major universities and chosen Dundee for his science because of the city's easy access to the Scottish mountains—mountaineering, along with marginal gardening and wildwater swimming, being one of his defining enthusiasms. He picked me up at Perth Railway station in a mud-spattered car. I wrote in a notebook, shortly after our meeting, that

He was a small wizened man with a parchment-wrinkled face. He wore a deerstalker hat and tall green wellingtons. He greeted me with instant familiarity—no shyness or reticence

continues on page 114

Poet-scientist G. F. Dutton, Perthshire, October 2007: 'I find Hardy's work depressing in that it's not human. A human must explore, it's like an animal out of a cage, it sniffs here and there, and if it doesn't want to sniff any more it's a dead animal. I've always sniffed as much as I could, beyond the cage. There are always new things to find out.'

The
Scottish-American
Poetry Magazine

16

The **Dark Horse**™

$5.00   £3.00

SPRING 2004

An issue which featured Diana Hendry's lively account of Ian Hamilton's posthumously published *Against Oblivion: Some Lives of the Twentieth-Century Poets*: mini-essays assessing the likelihood of particular poets' work surviving. This was also a 'First Books' issue, running reviews of twelve first books including those by Wilmer Mills, Matthew Fitt, Clive Watkins, Helena Nelson and A. B. Jackson.

The Scottish-American Poetry Magazine

17

The Dark Horse™

David Mason *Ted Kooser, American Laureate*
Helena Nelson *W. H. Davies Revisited*
Gerry Cambridge *Heavyweight Ted Hughes*
James Aitchison *On Poetry and Voice*
Alasdair D. F. Macrae *Yeats and Eternity*
G. F. Dutton *In Conversation*
John Ridland *A New Sir Gawain*
Kathleen McDermott *On Choman Hardi
and Catherine Tufariello*

Poems

Rose Kelleher, A. B. Jackson, Ann Stapleton, Ruth Silcock,
Joseph S. Salemi, Deborah Warren, A. E. Stallings, Elizabeth Burns

$5.00   £3.00
SUMMER 2005

This issue printed the little-known American poet Ann Stapleton's remarkable poem, 'Hail Maggie, Full of Grace', about a three-legged dog. The critic Kathleen McDermott contributed an intriguing review on first books by Choman Hardi and Catherine Tufariello, interestingly contrasting the Iraqui Kurd Hardi's less-polished poems on major subjects such as genocide among her own people with Tufariello's often elaborately formal poems on what the American poet Timothy Steele called 'the small ordinary decencies.' My own review was on Hughes' *Collected Poems*; though perhaps unfairly dubious about much of the myth-based work, it called him among other things 'the great poet of the trampish eccentric, or of unofficial human ingenuity on the tufted and unlegislated margins.'

whatever—and drove quickly. His speech too, was rapid, punctuated by chuckles and occasional incomprehensible mutterings and stutters. It was as if his thought processes operated with great rapidity and his speech made a passable attempt at keeping up: like a couple of foxes, one chasing the other through an intricate countryside. The thought-fox, of course, was invisible, but the voice-fox, so to speak, kept disappearing from view in thickets and along the hedges of his delivery before suddenly appearing in plain view again, crossing a field.

Dutton's spare, probing poems, bare and northern in tone and outlook, had been praised by Anne Stevenson. His *Selected, The Bare Abundance*, had recently appeared from Bloodaxe. Even as a personality he was remarkable: one was exposed to an intellect following the complexities of whatever presented itself to him, or whatever he found engaging, with a self-confidence purely in its own power. When I met him, though he was ill and failing, he was still intellectually striking; in his peak years, he must have been formidable.

He was fascinated by what he saw as the complementariness of human subjectivity and the 'objective' truths of science; together, he had decided, they made up a larger truth about reality than either in isolation.

He wrote beautifully on the nature of poetry as he saw it. His view of it was far from the Slutsky attitude evinced here a few pages ago. On a manuscript page printed with the interview he wrote:

> ... [Sorley] MacLean inferred that a poem needs wheels, wheels strong enough to carry its load; and my own poems, except when they instantaneously completed themselves, had their emerging structure assembled, taken down and reassembled several times until [each] gave evidence of wheels and being able to carry the half-formulated revelation; then a last tuning, and some 'magic', some Stevensian Angel—only dimly perceived or quite unforeseen—might wing up and settle on board, ensuring its completion. The Logical then leaps on the screen to the Supralogical, if we are fortunate. Contact has been made.

A New Seriousness:

2006–2015

It would be a year before the subsequent issue, 18, was published. It marked the beginning of a change in my attitude towards the journal in relation to Arts Council assistance. For
years the Horse had trundled along on around £3,000 ann-
ually. This barely paid for production costs. I began to feel this
was holding it back, as I was too busy with other freelancing
engagements and had no real incentive to give it more of my
time. I decided to apply for extra money, both to pay contributors, and myself and our US Assistant Editor a modest amount
for our editorial work. I phoned Gavin Wallace, who was then
Literature Director at the Scottish Arts Council. Gavin was old-
school, scholarly, gentlemanly, and out for quality, a man who
had lugged around boxes of another Scottish literary journal in
its earlier days, *Cencrastus*.

'Gavin,' I said, 'I've decided my attitude towards applying for
funding for the magazine has been holding it back. I'm going
to apply for more money.'

'At last,' he said.

Issue 18 was a bridge issue, which marked the end of one
stage of the magazine and the beginning of another. It was the
first to appear under our new funding dispensation—we were
fortunate to have been awarded additional funds—which
marked an increased regularity in the journal's appearance
and a new, professional attitude.

I had just finished a freelance literary design project and
used some of the things I'd learnt—not wholly successfully—
in elements of the new issue. From this point on, each cover
of the Horse would be individually designed, full colour, and
distinct from its predecessor. My developing interest in typography would also lead me to experiment with a variety of different settings and typefaces in search of the perfect internal
layout. For this issue, though, the house face remained Sabon.
(I gave a title, 'The Printed Snow', to a piece included about
W. S. Graham, by the poet-critic David Cameron. In 2015 I
re-used the title for my pamphlet from Happen*Stance* Press

on typography and typesetting for poetry. It took the editor so long to encourage *The Printed Snow* from me that we took to calling it, affectionately, *The Melting Slush*).

The entire middle section of issue 18 had to be reprinted before the magazine was bound (its 96 pages were composed of three 32pp sections, in three signatures) at a cost of several hundred pounds. This was because of two egregious errors in an essay I had written on George Mackay Brown. Ordinarily, I would have produced an *erratum* slip, but we already had one for a typo in the editorial. See page 121 for my attempt to add to the canon of *erratum* slip as facesaving addition. It was not the most auspicious of new beginnings, though the number opened with a new contributor, and a significant 'name', for the magazine: the Scottish poet and novelist Andrew Greig. Its prose included John Lucas on Louis Simpson, a poet I had met and been impressed by as a person in the US in 2000.

Simpson and I had talked about MacDiarmid's cottage, where I'd lived. It turned out that not only had he been there but had also interviewed the old poet at Brownsbank not long before his death. The interview was unpublished. I asked him to send me it to consider for the magazine. When, a few months later, the yellowing typescript, in Pica type, arrived, the New York typist had evidently had considerable problems transcribing MacDiarmid's Scottish Borders accent.

I asked the Scottish novelist and poet James Robertson, the first Brownsbank Fellow, if he would take a look at it. Like me, unfortunately, he felt it unpublishable. I returned it some time later to Simpson with an apologetic note.

A subtitle declared this to be the *'Collecteds'* issue: the books involved were Simpson's, Anne Stevenson's, W. S. Graham's, and George Mackay Brown's. All were the subjects of essay-reviews, the Horse's preference always being to allow authors considerable space in discussing major books. Though I had not printed a poem of my own in the Horse since issue 9/10, and only sporadically before that, I have felt no similar restrictions apply to contributions to the magazine by me in prose, and wrote the piece 'The Isle Full of Voices' on Brown's *Collected*. In it I was able to use my long familiarity both with this poet's work and the environment in which it was written, and our friendship. Scotland, topographically, is a wholly different matter from much of England. I sometimes enjoyed taking southern-based critics or taste-makers to task for their presumption of centrality.

Philip Larkin had left Brown out of his famous *Oxford Book of Twentieth Century English Verse* (1973) while including the lesser (though still interesting and rightly included) Orkney poet and conchologist Robert Rendall. So I took a passing shot at the famous poet-librarian:

> A trip to Orkney might have made him more sympathetic. Indeed, it's fun to imagine the urbane sophisticate Larkin relocated briefly among the bumptious gusts. The islands' physical environment exposes the visitor to radically different psychological weathers. There are few trees; you get used to winds, spectacular far huddlings and changing arrangements of cumuli, sea, horizons, and the vulnerability of the human. In the city, nature is temporarily in abeyance. Everything human can be regarded there as central. On an island, the elements impress on you your individual insignificance, although islanders often seem to possess a surer and quicker grasp of human nature, because everything is stripped bare in that environment. Unlike in cities, anonymity is difficult, if not impossible. Brown frequently set his poems either in a historical past simplified by distance or in what he found the more imaginatively amenable Orkney of his childhood. He had a Luddite streak which, at least as an aesthetic strategy, disapproved of 'progress', while enjoying some of its blandishments, such as TV. Yet the experience of even contemporary Orkney provides an enlightening backdrop to reading the poems.

One poem of Brown's I discussed, 'The Seven Houses', had been written a few years after Al Alvarez's then famous and influential anthology *The New Poetry*. I commented:

> [Brown's poem is] a grave sonorous elegy for John F. Kennedy in which the houses of the title are the seven ages of 'man'. Its register is unlike anything else in contemporary British verse.

[119]

continues on page 122

The Scottish-American Poetry Magazine

TS

18

The Dark Horse™

W. S. Graham's Printed Snow — DAVID CAMERON

The Tinkers and Lairds of
George Mackay Brown — GERRY CAMBRIDGE

Louis Simpson:
American Splendour — JOHN LUCAS

Anne Stevenson's
Way of Saying — MARCIA MENTER

The *Collecteds* Issue

POEMS:

ANNE STEVENSON
ANDREW GREIG
TIMOTHY MURPHY
ANN STAPLETON
DAVID MASON
MICHAEL CANTOR
CAROL STEVENS KNER

Summer
2006

$5.00
£3.00

Number 18, marked by a new flamboyance of cover design and a determination to keep to a regular twice-yearly schedule which we have fulfilled, more or less, ever since. I had obviously learned how to make curves in *InDesign*.

Opposite: the erratum slip as a literary genre. Though I was immensely annoyed at the time by this misprint—I take typos as a personal affront—I have come to see such corrective slips as potential creative additions to a publication.

Erratum

While not of the status of gloriously mortifying misprints such as the title of William Neill's review of Sorley MacLean's poetry, 'The Woods of Raasay', appearing as 'The Weeds of Raasay' in a Highland newspaper; or of a Scottish broadsheet's surely mischievous recension of Randall Jarrell's uncharacteristically generous observation that "a good critic is one who likes as much as possible as persuasively as possible" to "a good critic is one who *lies* [my italics] as much as possible as persuasively as possible", please note that "commissed" in paragraph four of my editorial should read "commissioned". We only commiss work without misprints. I am grudgingly amused to have perpetrated a verb new to the English language: "to commiss": to skulk out of sight unnoticed until that moment when your creator's embarrassment will be greatest.

Chary Cambridge
Editre
The Dank Hoarse

Here is the first stanza:

Man, you are at the first door.
The woman receives you.
The woman takes you in.
With joy she takes you in to her long hall.
The nine candles are burning.
Here with reptile and fish and beast
You dance in silence.
Here is the table with the first food.
This is the house of the womb.

It's a mode of address far from the then-prevailing dictats of British verse, promulgated in Al Alvarez's *The New Poetry* (1962), of a confessionalist mode revelatory of the extremisms in the self and in society. Brown was omitted from Alvarez's supposedly ground-breaking anthology. But while Alvarez's directives for a contemporary poetry are a mere note in literary history, Brown's poem still resonates as a living thing—a reassuring indication of the primacy of art over criticism.

A little magazine of any individuality is never happier than when in disagreement.

* * *

*Consolidating new beginnings—against prizes—typos &
trauma—a crack at Armitage's Gawain—Heaney responds
to a critic—Heaney's magnanimity*

The following three issues, 19, 20 and 21, appeared at six month intervals beginning in winter 2006/2007. They marked the Horse's return to a regular publishing schedule. The impression conveyed, typographically at least, was of austere seriousness, differentiated mainly by the ground colours of the cover card.

Issue 19 was a sober and authoritative dark grey, with white text and a touch of red. Issue 20 sported what the US scholar-poet James Matthew Wilson referred to at the time, amusingly, as 'radioactive green'—a striking bright lime, with dark purple lettering. For issue 21, I used a pure white ground, with the text a combination of green, purple and black. This cover also had the standard Horse logo doubled and mirrored like a reflection—the subtext being that of retrospection and self-scrutiny at 21. I had chosen, after considerable swithering, the renaissance typeface Bembo, though this was an earlier digital version which looked a bit emaciated compared to the robust old metal version. It was disappointing.

Issue 19's editorial kicked off in standard polemical style, being a critique of some of the journal's *bête-noires*: poetry prizes, specifically, in this instance, the Forward Prize, and the irksome centrality of London in such matters. The editorial concluded, loftily: 'Compared to the ground-bass of time, and this is especially so from Scotland, [such prizes] seem some-thing of an irrelevant tinkle.' It is all there: the animosity, the faith in posterity, the haughty Scottish 'distance', and the com-edic dismissiveness in that 'tinkle'.

One centrepiece of the issue was an extended interview with the distinguished Scottish poet Stewart Conn in his 70th year, along with some critical assessments, a couple of new poems, and a characteristically acute 'note' on one of Conn's poems, 'Angel with Lute', by the poet-critic James Aitchison. The poem itself was reprinted on the facing page.

There had been editorial changes which affected the issue's contents. The American poet Marcia Menter had joined the masthead, initially as a 'US Book Review Editor'; she would later become an 'Advisory Editor'. The journal had frequently published her distinctive poems and her lucid and snappi-ly written essays—the latter the product of her training as a senior editor for women's magazines such as *Redbook*. Such work had given her a concern for clarity and a no-nonsense approach to unnecessary obfuscation in critical prose about poetry. I had been schooled to some extent in a similar area, mass market magazines, via my early freelancing for *Reader's Digest*. I belittled this experience in my early twenties but in retrospect valued it. I had some sympathy with Marcia's outlook. We had first met in 2000 at the second West Chester Poetry Conference I attended. I asked her what she did for a living. 'I edit articles with titles like "Your Love-Map to His Body"', she said, a lightness which disguised not only a substantial intellect but a valuable outsider's view on the contemporary poetry scene.

Marcia had brought to my attention David Lehman's new edition of *The Oxford Book of American Poetry*, the successor to Richard Ellmann's classic 1976 volume which, around 1984, had first introduced me to the major American poets. I thought the book would be considerable enough to merit significant attention. So I commissioned *two* reviews: one by the British poet-critic Clive Watkins; one by the American poet R. S. Gwynn. These were intertextual in one direction: I showed Watkins' admirable, detailed review to Gwynn when it came in, so he could make reference to it in his own piece.

Consideration of this major anthology took up the first twelve prose pages of issue 19. Both reviews were models of their type: scholarly, yet addressing a non-academic interested audience; critical, questioning, and with an impressive overview of the field. A major problem indicated by Watkins—his piece was titled 'Oxford's Addled Anthology'—was the number of misprints. He wrote:

> A few figures will suggest the scale of the problem. In the first 566 pages, I detect errors on sixty-four pages. Some pages have more than one error; one has six. Of the eighty-nine poets represented in those pages, twenty-one—that is, 24%—have had at least one error inflicted on them. Some suffer more badly than others. Of the twenty-one pages given to Bishop six contain errors; of Eliot's thirty-two and a half pages, thirteen contain errors; of Pound's fifteen pages, seven contain errors: that is, 29%, 40% and 47% respectively of the pages devoted to these poets.
>
> Many errors are startlingly obvious—or so one might have thought. In Robinson's 'Luke Havergal', the protagonist's name is spelled correctly on every occasion save the last, where it appears as 'Like Havergal'. In the third line of Elinor Wylie's 'Wild Peaches', 'Abroad' appears as 'Aborad'. Wystan

Hugh Auden is re-christened 'Wynstan', an error doubtless influenced by the homophone 'Winston'.

Other errors are more insidious and therefore more likely to catch the unwary. Line three of Frost's 'Mending Wall' appears thus: 'And spills upper boulders in the sun', but while this might slip past a reader whose metrical sense was poor, what Frost wrote was a regular decasyllabic pentameter: 'And spills the upper boulders in the sun'. (Though it is not a typographical error, Lehman adopts Lathem's notorious re-punctuation of 'The woods are lovely, dark and deep', inserting a comma after 'dark', thereby changing the pace and sense of the line.) In Stevens's 'The Man Whose Pharynx Was Bad', Lehman gives the middle lines of stanza three as follows: 'Perhaps, if winter once could penetrate / Through all its purples to the final state'. This makes sense and rhymes, but what Stevens wrote was not 'state' but the more striking and much less predictable 'slate'. In Canto XIII two lines are repeated; a line is dropped from Canto LXXXI. In 'Little Gidding' 'Then fools' approval stings' is given as 'The fools' approval stings'. Many lines are incorrectly spaced. And so on, and so on. Spotting misprints in familiar poems is one thing. But how, in reading an unfamiliar poem, especially one that plays tricks with conventional usage, is one to be sure that its text can be relied upon? And this of course casts a shadow over the reliability of the entire volume.

This allowed Gwynn, a wittily sardonic and voluminously-read poet-critic, to begin by riffing on amusing typographical howlers he had known. They included the notorious added definite article to the last line of Edward Arlington Robinson's sonnet, about the butcher, 'Reuben Bright', as it had appeared in Robinson's second collection, *Children of the Night*:

> And after she was dead, and he had paid
> The singers and the sexton and the rest,
> He packed a lot of things that she had made
> Most mournfully away in an old chest
> Of hers, and put some chopped-up cedar boughs
> In with them, and tore down to the slaughter-house.

Robinson's grievous portrayal of Reuben Bright's outlook-changing response to his wife's death—he *tore down* the slaughter-house' [my italics]—becomes here the character's preposterous acceleration in a puff of dust to the dubious building, much like the Roadrunner in the old Hanna-Barbera cartoons.

David Lehman, the Oxford book's editor, emailed me to ask for Watkins' email contact, to ask if Watkins might supply a list of the errors he had discovered so they could be corrected in further printings. Watkins, however, had since destroyed his notes. Perhaps, too, he did not feel inclined to act as unpaid proofreader for OUP America. For my part, I savoured the rich irony by which a little magazine like the Horse was able to point out to a major publishing house that a significant anthology under its imprint was thrang with errors.

* * *

The element of contention continued in the subsequent number, issue 20. It is fascinating to commission authoritative reviews by writers who know the subject under review inside out. One such was Mary Veazey, a remarkable woman in her sixties looking after her aged mother and living at times for respite in a caravan in Maplesville, Alabama. Poetry has a habit of throwing up remarkable individualists, and she was one. Her emails to me contained accounts of tornado warnings and occasional illness—she kept in poor health—but were generally sprightly, rather Thoreau-ish affairs.

Mary was an enthusiast for the great anonymous medieval poem *Sir Gawain and the Green Knight*. She had been helping the California poet John Ridland with his own translation. Faber had just published in the UK Simon Armitage's version of this masterpiece, but its cover design, playing up to the ignorance of many a contemporary reader, appeared to suggest that the translator was the author. Veazey observed:

[A] confusing statement is Armitage's remark in his introduction in regard to the Gawain poet: 'The lack of authorship
seems to serve as an invitation, opening up a space within the
poem for a new writer to occupy.' 'Anonymous' in no way con-
stitutes 'lack of authorship.' This was a real person, a man in
all probability because it's difficult to imagine a woman of that
time lingering so obsessively over the hunting and slaughter-
ing of the deer, boar, and fox, in Part III, at the castle where
Gawain takes refuge. There's a space within the poem for a
translator, but the space for the author is taken by an unknown
genius whose mastery deserves full acknowledgement.

An example will serve to show the level of Mary Veazey's attention, which is a form of love. Here is a small section of the
Armitage. The italics are hers:

> 'But enough at New Year. It needs nothing more,'
> said the *war-man* in green to worthy Gawain.
> 'I could tell you the truth *once you've taken the blow;*
> if you smite me smartly I could spell out the facts
> of my house and home and my name, *if it helps,*
> then you'll pay me a visit and vouch for our pact.
> *Or if I keep quiet* you might cope much better,
> *loafing and lounging here*, looking no further....'

(ll. 404–11)

First, there is no 'war-man' in the original line 405. In line
406 Armitage's Green Knight says, 'I could tell you the truth
once you've taken the blow,' implying that the real truth will
come out after Gawain has taken the blow in a year and a
day. But it is the Green Knight who is to receive the blow: the
original says 'Yif I the telle trwly quen I the tape have,' loosely,
'If I tell you faithfully, when I've taken the blow.' Got to get
the right head beheaded! The tail end of line 408, 'if it helps,'
is not in the original and seems to imply that the information the Green Knight will provide to Gawain is worthless.
Armitage's putting 'Or if I keep quiet' (after the blow) in the
Green Knight's mouth is quite similar to the original's 'And if I
spende no speche,' except that 'keep quiet' implies a conscious

effort to avoid speaking, whereas the original seems an understated euphemism for death. Lines 410 and 411 translate, then, as follows: 'And if I say nothing, it will work out better for you, because you may remain in your country and seek no further.' Armitage's substitution of 'loafing and lounging here' for 'may remain' is rather insulting to Gawain and the court, and not justified translation.

Mary Veazey never wrote again for the Horse. She died of *myasthenia gravis*, which had been diagnosed just two months earlier, on November 13, 2009.

The issue was spiritedly disputatious elsewhere. The poet, critic and clinical neuropsychologist Séan Haldane, another enthusiast, this time for Gaelic, offered a piece on the English 'versions' of the Gaelic originals of the great poet Sorley MacLean. The general point of his essay was that Sorley's own English translations are definitive and superior to those, so far, of anyone else.

In the course of his piece he chose Seamus Heaney's 2002 version of MacLean's astonishing poem about the Highland Clearances, 'Hallaig', for criticism, and in some detail. He had considerable sport with the Heaney translation:

> Passing by the substitution of 'lightheaded' for 'dizzily', as if the deer had been at a cocktail party, why the unjustified Anglo Saxon 'wallsteads'? The Scots Gaelic word 'larach' simply means 'a building in ruins.' Its equivalent in Irish Gaelic, 'lathair' means an empty space, a site. Its root 'lar' means simply 'floor' in Scots Gaelic (Irish Gaelic 'urlar'). It is cognate with the Latin 'lar' meaning 'hearth'. It suggests houses ruined down to their floors and their burned out hearths.
>
> Etymology is not everybody's meat, but a really careful translation like MacLean's includes a word by word awareness of it. An original poem is likely to resonate on several levels of word meaning and word origins. This resonance on multiple levels is what makes a poem untranslatable except into prose.

By the time a poet is as famous as Heaney was when this was written, he rarely gets such candour about anything he has published. I sent Seamus this issue with a sinking heart. He had been a considerable supporter not only of my own work but of the Horse since issue 2.

I wrote that if he wished to make a response to the criticisms I would publish it in the subsequent issue. (With editorial hat on, you are always thinking strategically: 'Seamus Heaney Responds to His Critic' would have made a great cover headline.) Some three weeks later a thick white envelope addressed in his handwriting thudded onto my doormat. I opened it. It was a print out of something he thought would interest me from a US magazine, on the change to reading culture brought about by the internet (a subject my editorial had addressed), plus a letter praising aspects of the journal.

He graciously turned down a public response to Haldane. 'The only thing I'd say,' he added, is that i) the final stanzas [of 'Hallaig'] seem to me a bit of a puzzle at the best of times; ii) my version was what he commends in general, a 'private homage to the poet'—advocacy and dissemination being the point and iii) that being the case, I thought he went on a bit.'

The letter also contained a cheque for 500 euros partly for 'personal refreshment and reward'. I briefly thought of writing to him jokily that, if a couple of paragraphs of criticism resulted in such largesse, what might an essay of similar severity, or a whole issue of it, even, be worth?

His was a deft response to criticism: a gesture both of magnanimity in the face of opprobrium and aid for the journal, indirectly making it less likely the Horse would run anything critical again on his work. He must also have known that it would make a good story in the retelling—as has proved the case. That all these things are simultaneously true does not, to my mind, diminish the magnanimity of the act. After all, he could simply have ignored the magazine.

Apart from Seán Haldane's three or four paragraphs, we never ran an essay on Seamus's work in the entire history of the Horse. My thinking was that he simply didn't need it. The Horse's limited extent is better used to highlight less well known but equally interesting figures. Throughout the journal's history, and making allowance for writing on poets in whom there is considerable curiosity among the poetry world, I have always been keen to run, alongside such assessments, pieces about neglected or lesser-known poets whose work merits it. As the journal's 'mission statement' (insofar as we can be said to have a 'mission') puts it: we wish to honour literary quality, not literary fashion. Poetry is a long game. This or that prizewinning sensation of the moment may or may not go on to real and sustained achievement; in any case, the Horse prefers to make its own mind up. Our own judgements and faith in our own sensibilities, as poets but also as poetry readers and critics, are finally all we have. They are not to be given up for the sake of a respectable alliance with a generally-held opinion. For this reason the journal has tended not to run notices of poets being roundly praised all around us; we would only devote space to such work if the critic had something unusual or critical to say that few others appeared to be saying. Otherwise, we often devote our pages to interesting work unlikely to win a prize or receive 'mainstream' attention. (That said, 'mainstream' is a misnomer in contemporary poetry: even the mainstream is a trickling rivulet in the more capacious waters of the general culture.)

* * *

A discovery—an elegy—unsolicited Matthew Sweeney

And it was to a writer far less known that the next issue, 21, devoted a good deal of attention. Any little magazine of distinction receives a lot of copies for review. The number of volumes of new poetry published is large; the number of reviewers willing to take time over a book, and the amount of space available in the print journals, small. Quite often an editor doesn't have time to even glance at new review copies as they arrive. You are exposed to such a weight of new work that, in darker moments, it can devalue the whole enterprise of poetry.

One day, though, the admirable Bloodaxe sent me *Transgressions: Selected Poems*, by Jack Gilbert. I had never heard of him—unusual for me, but this was in the far bigger field of American poetry, after all. For some reason, perhaps because the first poem or two I sampled gripped and intrigued me, I read the book more closely: caught, I think, by the undodging directness of the voice and the subject matter. A number of the poems dealt with his grief after the death of his young Japanese wife, Michiko Nogami. He was, more generally, a love poet.

As I have got older, my taste both in reading poems and in what I aspire to write myself has tended away from the ludic towards a poetry stripped bare, even when written in persona, of affectation: a simplified writing of plain statement, but a simplicity achieved having passed *through* complexity, not halting before it.

Gilbert, in his best pieces, seemed to have attained such a voice. I thought highly enough of his writing to track down and buy a hardback copy of perhaps his finest book, *The Great Fires* (memorably set by the New York publishing house Knopf in American type designer W. A. Dwiggins' typeface Electra).

I assigned two notices. One was by Marcia Menter—who I felt would resonate strongly with Gilbert's straightforward statements on the life of the spirit. The other was by Jesse Rossa, now a rare book dealer, who contributed an anecdotal piece describing Jack Gilbert readings he'd attended. Via the poet Henry Lyman, who dealt with literary matters for Gilbert in his later life, I had obtained three new Jack Gilbert poems.

While the issue celebrated the living, it also featured a commemoration of the dead: the poet-critic Eva Salzman contributed a fiercely personal yet scholarly memoir of her friend and colleague Sarah Hannah, who took her own life at the age of 41.

This number marked notable debut appearances in the Horse by two poets. One was Tom Duddy, a singular Irish writer with a background in philosophy, who wrote intriguingly on his rural background but in a way which did much more than conjure Heaney. Duddy was barely known. The other poet was the widely published Matthew Sweeney, whose poem 'Dwarves' was a strange, comic revisiting of Yeats' 'Byzantium'. His poems had arrived unsolicited. It is always a fine thing when a better known poet, something of a 'name', submits work to a little magazine. Not only is it a mark of respect for the journal but it displays a refreshing lack of expectation or tacit entitlement on behalf of the poet: the absence of one of the less pleasant aspects of poetic ego.

* * *

A little known sonneteer—editing from judgement—poetry in the postmodern age

Despite its bright yellow cover, and red and black (though still sober and restrained) typography, issue 22 from August 2008 was perhaps a transitional issue, of sorts. Its prose contributions revisited some habitual Horse interests—X. J. Kennedy, Frost, Edward Thomas, the letters of Ted Hughes. There was a fascinating account of Belli translations by the poet-critic Peter Robinson, which used as its donnée a new book of Belli versions by a remarkable younger writer then living in Edinburgh, Mike Stocks. He was obsessed with the sonnet and his own poems were all in this form. (His book of distinctive sonnets, *Folly*, attracted little critical attention and is not widely known. Issued by the small press Herla in 2006, its best poems have an achieved and stark simplicity; a number of them had previously appeared in the Horse.)

By far the longest piece, in this issue, at 17 pages, was the young critic Hannah Brooks-Motl's 'Gentle and Come Ouer': The Role of the Reader in Contemporary Poetry'. Her piece attempted admirably to come to grips, via selected examples, with contemporary postmodern American poetry. She tackled this with a lot more patience than I would have shown. My publishing the essay was an occasional example of my editing, as least in the prose, from 'judgement' rather than 'personal taste'. This distinction is not mine, but Michael Schmidt's. The implication is that the former is more 'objective' than the latter, but I am not wholly convinced. Put more straightforwardly, it

[132]

continues on page 137

The
Scottish–American
Poetry Magazine

19

WINTER
2006 / 2007

An extensive interview with Stewart Conn and essays and appreciations on his poetry helped marked his 70th birthday. The excellent poet Robert Nye appeared in the Horse for the first time here; he once remarked to me, apropos poetry prizes, that the thing was to be so far away from winning such a prize that it was never even a consideration. Wilmer Mills, a remarkable poet whom I'd met at the West Chester Poetry Conference, also appeared in the magazine for the first time. (He died at the age of 41 in 2011.) This cover marked the beginning of a run of four covers featuring austere design and typography. The typefaces here are Bembo and Trajan.

The
Scottish-American
Poetry Magazine

20

SUMMER 2007

For some reason, this issue sold particularly well in retail outlets—perhaps down to its spectacular green. The typeface again is Bembo. Both the Veazey and the Haldane essays were high-level critiques which brought an acute and fearless eye to the versions they were discussing. Shamelessly biased as I must own up to being, I think these essays of permanent value.

E. A. Robinson: A Life
Reading Robert Garioch
Jack Gilbert, American Poet
Norman MacCaig's Clear Eye
Ars Longa, Vita Brevis: On Sarah Hannah
The Dark Horse at 21

Poems:

Kevin Cutrer
Rachel Hadas
Diana Hendry
Andrew Hudgins
Sydney Lea
Matthew Sweeney
Catherine Tufariello

The Scottish-American
Poetry Magazine

The
Dark
Horse

Winter 2007/2008 | 21

Issue 21, with titling typography in Myriad Pro, a typeface designed by Robert Slimbach. I was especially proud of our reflected logo.

The Scottish-American
Poetry Magazine
The Dark Horse

22

Yellow did not seem to go down particularly well with retail buyers, as this issue sold less well than usual in such outlets, or perhaps the cover typography was too austere. Electra Small Caps for the titling, with Requiem fleurons.

differentiates between an editor who publishes something because s/he thinks it should be published, and one who prints only things s/he finds personally engaging. It is too easy for me to read 'editing from judgement' as a means of outwitting accountability for one's choices. All editorial selection takes place in a continuum between those two positions. I thought Brooks-Motl most interesting in her forbearance in attempting to comprehend particular poems and poetries I would have peremptorily dismissed, life being short enough.

There is a long discussion to be had about whether we should read poetry with any more tolerance than we show for novels which, if we find unengaging, we put aside without ceremony. To what extent should a reader of poetry *make allowance?* Sometimes one feels that a good deal of contemporary verse is read with a sort of dutiful and politically correct respect. Like a form of medicine, it is meant to be good for you in the enlargement of spirit it offers, however unmemorably. I do not find publishing from judgement particularly satisfying.

* * *

Design adventurousness—typography & the renaissance aristocrat—the beauty of Richard Wilbur—Kirsch & criticism—a new Indian-American poet—gossipy Menashe

If issue 22, from late summer 2008, was something of a transition, the next three numbers, 23 to 25, marked a move towards a new design adventurousness on the cover. From here on, every cover would be a sort of 'project'. Issue 22 had used Robert Slimbach's Arno Pro as its text face; the next three numbers were set in Poliphilus and its companion italic Blado. Characterised by its upward slanting hyphen, this renaissance typeface has been described by the poet-typographer Robert Bringhurst as 'a rough, somewhat rumpled yet charming face, like a Renaissance aristocrat, unshaven and in stockinged feet, caught between the bedroom and the bath.'

There was a new, lively note to these issues, perhaps influenced by recent positive developments in my private life and evident in my editorial for issue 23 (see page 140). The number not only ran one of the most beautiful essays in the history of the magazine, D. M. Black's 'Reflections on a Poem by Richard Wilbur'—a model of sensitive reading and attention—but also Tom Duddy's essay making a case that the modesty of Thomas Hardy as a poet was part of what constituted his 'strange greatness'. It bore as an epigraph this observation by Hardy: 'I fear I have always been considered the *Dark Horse* of Contemporary English Literature.'

Less of an essay, more a review, less formal and yet still scholarly, was A. E. Stallings' spritely account of Edward Hirsch and Eavan Boland's *The Making of a Sonnet*; Stallings, a formal virtuoso, was its ideal reviewer. I was also particularly happy to run a notice of Adam Kirsch's *The Modern Element*—brief essays on contemporary poets, reminiscent of Michael Schmidt's *An Introduction to 50 Modern British Poets*. Kirsch's were pithy, witty and not altogether laudatory accounts. They interested even when they appeared wrong-headed—as they did quite often to the fine critic Mario Relich, who reviewed them.

And the issue opened with eleven pages of new poems by the young Indian-American poet Amit Majmudar. He had first appeared—his inaugural publication in a UK literary journal, I believe—in issue 20. Majmudar is a poet of wide-ranging themes and intelligence. His work is remarkable not only for its formal dexterity but for its filtering of contemporary themes—at that point, the Iraq War—through his own sensibility as a modern Indian man living in America. This is further filtered through his outlook as a Hindu with a wide-ranging interest in Western religion. As he is also a diagnostic nuclear radiographer, Majmudar crosses the traditional art/science divide. All this brings a new mix to contemporary English-language poetry. Though Don Paterson has compared him (intriguingly, to my mind) with Thomas Hardy, to me his work is closer to Derek Walcott crossed with a restless experimenter such as Edwin Morgan. Like Walcott in the early days, who in a sonnet sequence such as 'Tales from the Islands' fills a traditional form with new, exhilarating subject matter from his native Caribbean, Majmudar will sometimes cross-fertilise an older literary style or model with unexpected content drawn from his wide range of concerns and interests. (So, for instance, his poem 'The Autobiography of Khwaja Mustasim' features a fictitious character talking of his many physical existences down through history, ending in the painful present. It echoes a famous Irish Gaelic poem by the mediaeval Irish bard Amergin.) As Edwin Morgan did, too, Majmudar will frequently project himself into other existences. He seldom writes direct autobiography. When I commented on this to the English poet-editor Lavinia Singer, who edits *Oxford Poetry*, she wondered if the writing served as a distancing from difficult medical elements involved in this poet's occupation.

* * *

Assembling any issue, sometimes themes and connections present themselves. As with writing one's own poetry, it can be fascinating to discover poems 'talking' to each other, and making further links with prose in the issue. *The Dark Horse* 24 began with two poems by women, Kathryn Jacobs and Lisa Williams, on difficult sexual encounters—one more oblique, the other a terse, plain narrative, and both exceptional. The focus on women's writing continued: the issue's reviews included lengthy considerations of a new anthology, *Women's Work: Modern Women Poets Writing in English*, edited by Eva Salzman and Amy Wack, and of new books by Sharon Olds as well as a biography of Ruth Pitter. As the Horse has matured, I have felt it more important to encourage critical writing by women. Two of these reviews were by female critics, though the Olds was by Mario Relich. The issue's interview with that poet of gnomic minimalism, Samuel Menashe, was conducted by our US editors, Marcia Menter and Jennifer Goodrich. A decided lady's man, Menashe, then in his eighties, flourished under their attention. His conversation is at once gossipy,

continues on page 143

The Dark Horse Editorial

TED HUGHES ONCE used a startling and implacably Darwinian metaphor in describing the various niches and styles poets adopt, whether consciously or not, in order to ensure some chance of survival for their work. The idea that poets are refined, higher souls indifferent to such matters as their position in any presumed pecking order or league table, or to publicity, is one soon scotched by an intimate involvement with the art. All poets therefore contain a paradox: the relatively self-less, open sensibility out of which poems get written, and the significant ego that all poets must have, if you scratch them a little, not only to think their work worth publishing but to try to get it published whether in venues famous or obscure. It can be a difficult thing to reconcile within one's self. Behind any poet who has achieved a reputation is likely to be a sense of strategy as, at some level, all poets want to be read or, at least, accorded recognition for having accomplished something within a difficult literary art.

Not that self-promotion is necessarily a negative thing. Stevie Smith has a poem, 'The Weak Monk', in which the central character writes a theological work about 'God and men' but, out of a sense of expectation 'that God / would rescue his book alive from the sod', buries it in the earth. The rain and snow rots it in the ground. Smith's poem concludes, pithily, 'For this the monk is to blame.' I suppose one moral of this could be that, where putting your work before the public is concerned, don't leave anything to Fate.

Notions like this, which belong to the practical, worldly, politic flip side of the business of writing poems are much in my mind reading both Julie Kane on the Salzman/Wack *Women's Work* anthology in this issue—a book which is surely a remarkable labour of love—and the certainly not self-abnegating sparky interview with Samuel Menashe. Anthologies, for one, are traditionally entry points into poetry for the curious and, with no derogation implied, the ignorant, with all the responsibility that that entails. One thing that cannot be said about *Women's Work*, as it ostensibly can about other anthologies, is that it is a product of laziness or partial ignorance. One thing that cannot be said about Samuel Menashe is that he will be an agent of his poems rotting in the ground.

Some of the swooning aberrations that poets' fear of languishing un-read can lead to, in an age of hype and advertising, are flagged up by Dennis O'Driscoll in a spirited polemic, 'Blurbonic Plague', coming up in issue 25. See page 95 of this issue for a preview.

Like poets, poetry magazines, too, show this 'flip side' writ large. Pub-lished with passion, as they ought to be, indeed, like bigger versions of those poems that form much of their content, each of them sings, in its own way, in poetry's tree, and the song says—let it be shamelessly—*'I am! I am!'*

Above: issue 23's editorial.

Opposite, top: a bit more cover flamboyance for the cover of number 23. Poliphilus Small Caps for the titling, with Requiem fleurons marked out in red.
Opposite, below: Richard Wilbur's characteristically equable and courteous response to D. M. Black's marvellous essay on one of his poems.

The Scottish-American Poetry Magazine

The Dark Horse 23

HARDY'S RADICAL MODESTY ❧ TOM DUDDY

ADAM KIRSCH AND CRITICISM ❧ MARIO RELICH

THE LOST LEADER ❧ N. S. THOMPSON

SONNET WORLD ❧ A. E. STALLINGS

AMERICAN POETRY AND 9/11 ❧ KENNETH SHERMAN

THE POETRY OF WALKING ❧ CHRISTIAN McEWEN

RICHARD WILBUR'S 'ELSEWHERE' ❧ D. M. BLACK

POEMS:

AMIT MAJMUDAR   HELENA NELSON   ROBERT NYE

LINDA CHASE   SEBASTIAN BARKER   KATRINA NAOMI

Summer 2009

RICHARD WILBUR

3 August 2009

Editors,
The Dark Horse

    Sirs:

        I want to thank you for your kindness
in sending me your latest issue, which contains
the essay on my work by D. M. Black. I am
grateful not only for Mr. Black's encouragement, but also for the tact and insight with
which he reads me. Many good wishes to you
and to your fine magazine,

                        Richard Wilbur

The Scottish-American
Poetry Magazine 24

Winter 2009 / 2010

POEMS:

ELIZABETH BURNS

JAMES CUMMINS

DAVID KINLOCH

ANGELA LEIGHTON

AMIT MAJMUDAR

CHARLES MARTIN

LISA WILLIAMS

WOMEN'S WORK ❧ JULIE KANE

DONAGHY THE MAGICIAN ❧ DAVID MASON

THE POETRY OF IAN HAMILTON
❧ MARCUS SMITH

FORGOTTEN RUTH PITTER
❧ HELENA NELSON

SAMUEL MENASHE IN CONVERSATION

SHARON OLDS AND THE BODY
❧ MARIO RELICH

THE STRANGE CASE
OF MARTIN SEYMOUR-SMITH ❧ DAVID CAMERON

The **Dark Horse**

The fine Scottish poet David Kinloch appeared in the magazine for the first time in issue 24, with a remarkable poem in Cockney about the gay artists Colquhoun and MacBryde being visited by a highly suspicious policeman. David Cameron and Helena Nelson brought new light to bear on two neglected figures, and David Mason wrote about his friend, the Irish-American poet Michael Donaghy, who died at the age of 50 in 2004. I had encountered Donaghy a few times, and read with him at the launch of the British edition of *The Hudson Review* in London in 2000; he appeared, as if by magic, from nowhere two minutes before the reading was due to begin, and performed from memory his remarkable poem 'Black Ice and Rain'.

humane, a touch vengeful with the edge of the marginalised, and erudite. Here he is on literary life:

> I'll tell you about a traumatic experience. I was a colleague of Anthony Hecht at Bard College. And Anthony Hecht, may he rest in peace, was three years older than I and a graduate of Bard and had just come back with the Prix de Rome. We were young instructors and thought we were friends, but soon enough we didn't like each other. He never said anything spontaneous in his life; he was the most *mindful* person. Once somebody brought me to a party at [anthologist and poet] Oscar Williams's, which I never would have been invited to on my own. As I stepped out onto the big penthouse roof, Anthony Hecht saw me and his jaw dropped, and he said, 'What are *you* doing here?' I still to this day think there are certain parties I'm brought to where people are saying that.

Menashe died in August 2011, some three weeks short of his 86th birthday. Although he achieved some late recognition in the US in 2004 via The Poetry Foundation's 'Neglected Masters Award', a large swathe of poetry readers in the UK, it may fairly be surmised, have never heard of him.

* * *

The Horse gets carnaptious—blurbitis—a new website—bless the critics, unafraid—the perils of criticism

Possibly the most polemical issue of the magazine ever, issue 25, appeared in July 2010. It included Dennis O'Driscoll's exasperated 'Blurbonic Plague', which he was worried the great *Poetry Daily* website would want to highlight as its 'Prose Feature of the Week': he feared a backlash from the (predominantly American) blurb writers featured in his polemic. Here he is in good-humoured overdrive:

> There are blurbs which deck out the poet in prophet's robes: 'It is a bleak and dangerous time for all mankind. And yet, we shall, despite horrendous evidence, prevail and survive—and

hopefully, grow as we glow on hearing his eloquent tribute to our species.' And if one poet reminds us that 'we are each still newly placed among the living', another will marry 'the passionate grief of *By Grand Central Station I Sat Down and Wept* with the pared-down utterances of Beckett's lost men' or 'draw you into her lines like a spider on hyper-spin'. Hyper-spin indeed! And hats off to the poet who 'does not merely write a poem, she wrenches it into being, slaps it on the page, applies the flames of her passions, then gentles it into the sweating fleshy sweetness of childhood hungers, longings inspired by loneliness or loss, starkly erotic yearnings—all served in deliciously monstrous portions, to be savored like a long slow French, that perfect tongue of a kiss that sets the soul on throb.' The kissing continues on another besotted cover: a collection whose author, having been 'kissed by the lips of eternity', 'managed to remain lucid enough to speak of the wonder'. Such conversation-stopping blurbs are a kiss of death—a more chaste and continent cover would show greater dignity and credibility.

The issue also ran John Lucas's disenchanted piece on the recent Bloodaxe anthology *Identity Parade*—featuring 85 younger poets and edited by Roddy Lumsden. I like to assign books about which honest opinions may not be forthcoming to more senior, less easily impressed critics. They blow through the smothering hype around much current poetry, which is often mutually congratulatory, like a gust of January air through a mim-moue'd cocktail party. It is not that such critics are deliberately combative; they are merely unafraid. Fear of creating offence is a major issue in the contemporary poetry world, which is a relatively small boat; rock it, and you may be thrown overboard. And there is no large, popular readership to be validated by; there is only the sea.

Some critics of course enjoy, indeed relish, swimming—one might characterise them, in this metaphor, as great whites—and don't find the water uncongenial. Issue 25 also featured the young poet-critic Rory Waterman—a judicious but by no means uncritical voice—on that champion swimmer and naysayer, William Logan. Writing in the *New Criterion* and elsewhere, Logan appears to revel in being almost programmatically dismissive. Invariably amusing and interesting to read, he can nonetheless appear utterly wrong-headed when one knows the poet/work which, as most often, he is dismissing. This is so in his derisory view of the Second World War poet Keith Douglas, dead in battle at 24.

These were uncertain times. The recession of late 2008/ 2009 had hit. Its aftershocks were affecting funding for the arts. Two long-running Scottish literary journals, *Lallans* and *Markings*—the latter had begun in the same year as *The Dark Horse*—received 100% funding cuts from Creative Scotland, effectively shutting them down. It was perfectly possible that the Horse would follow.

Most little magazines of any distinction are underfunded. The editor ends up being a jack of all trades. S/he is likely to be strong on editorial matters, weak on marketing. I also have considerable design and typographic skills, but marketing was never my strong suit. (I have, though, small patience for the idea of the poet as useless at everything else bar writing poetry: I think poets can do almost anything they set their minds to, within reason.) Up till the winter of 2009/2010— it seems remarkable to think of this now—the Horse didn't even possess a fully functioning website. Around 2003 I had come to an arrangement with the *Star* Project at Edinburgh University, under Professor Susan Manning, which promoted transatlantic literary connections. I had convinced them that it was within their remit to host some rudimentary web pages for the magazine. But readers could not subscribe online. Subscribers, whether US or UK, had to pay by cheque. The first rule of selling being 'put as few obstacles between a buyer and what they want as possible,' this lack of an online subscription facility was a major obstacle to new readers. Accordingly, and helped that winter by a substantial Writer's Bursary for my own work, I decided to learn some website building skills and built a new Horse website from scratch, complete with archives, updates—and a Paypal purchasing facility. In this sense, a journal such as the Horse may have an effect on its editor much like evolutionary pressures on an organism in

The Scottish-American
Poetry Magazine

The
**Dark
Horse**

25

Summer / Autumn 2010

IDENTITY PARADE: JOHN LUCAS ON BLOODAXE'S NEW ANTHOLOGY

ANNE STEVENSON ON NEW AMERICAN POETS

JOHN GREENING ON JAMES MERRILL

DENNIS O'DRISCOLL: BLURBONIC PLAGUE

RORY WATERMAN: SAVAGE ART: WILLIAM LOGAN'S CRITICISM

HELENA NELSON ON FOUR SENIOR MASTERS; CHARLOTTE NEWMAN ON THREE FIRST BOOKS

POEMS: ROBERT NYE, ANNEMARIE AUSTIN, ANDREW GREIG, JOHN PURSER, AMIT MAJMUDAR

'Scotland's finest
international literary journal.
And, oddly enough, one
of the most consistently
interesting journals on
American poetry.'
—Dana Gioia

The only occasion on which a photograph has featured on the front cover, this was my image of some notebooks vertically stretched, isolated in Photoshop, and with the magazine's Contents highlights added to the notebook spines. These included a review of 'Four Senior Masters', one of whom was the late lamented Alexander (Sandy) Hutchison, who took me to task at the time for the word 'senior' in relation to himself. Anne Stevenson wrote beautifully on the *Swallow Anthology of Younger American Poets* ('Swallow' as in the bird) with major praise, coming from her, of A. E. Stallings in particular.

the natural world. Through natural selection, those pressures refine favourable genetic mutations in an individual of a particular species: you are forced to learn things you otherwise wouldn't. *The Dark Horse* entered the modern age. As with its appearance on social media from 2011, this had an almost immediate, beneficial effect on subscriptions and sales.

* * *

The Horse and maturity—typographic finesse—
the pizzazz of the cover—Kay Ryan on rhyming—
Dennis O'Driscoll, gentleman

The Horse entered its maturity, I like to think, from around number 26 (Autumn/Winter 2010) to the present (2016). It is not my intention to write an issue-by-issue account of the journal to date, but I will mention highlights and perhaps point out some general trends. The magazine is now firmly established as one of the longer-running poetry journals, well known both in the UK and the US, featured from time to time in other publications such as *The Times Literary Supplement*, the great *Poetry Daily* website in the US, and the foremost journal for creative writing in the US, *Poets & Writers*. I believe it is one of the most stringently edited journals, for a little magazine, that I know of. Assigned prose goes through thorough copy-editing and checking; suggested edits are marked up using the editing features in Microsoft Word and sent to the author for approval, query, or debate. I now insist on receiving two review copies of any book being given review space. Writers can be extraordinarily slapdash—I realise, from my own experience of writing criticism—in the accuracy of their quotations from source texts, so all quotations are checked against their originals. Once a final edit has been agreed, the finished essay or review is typeset and then proofed again both in-house and by the author. The process is less intensive in poetry, where my suggested edits are far fewer, when they exist at all. I like to think the journal's editorial standards are at least as rigorous—perhaps more so—as that of any major publishing house. (That said, in a time of poor editorial standards, this might not be such an impressive claim.)

* * *

Issues 26 to the present have been marked by their covers' bold typographic designs and, hopefully, distinguished inner typography. Issue 26, with its—for my money—classy combination of black, red and grey on a cream cover, and complex though simple-seeming setting in Hypatia Sans with (modified) Grafika, even made it into the *TLS*'s 'NB' column of March 11, 2011. The NB page's one featured graphic was a scan of the cover, with a note from the column's writer, James Campbell, quoting my letter to him about the design. Such design considerations also marked my increasing awareness— manifested around the same time by the book trade—that publications could be beautiful objects in their own right, with a physical presence no e-book could ever match. Our logo, which had remained a constant from issue 1, survived untouched in its original form until issue 29. Then, for the first time, I separated the Horse, which I had decided was the part of the original design most associated with the journal, into a free-floating element. Issue 29 even featured *two* horses in a decorative design where they bookended the central display-text block. Generally, the Horse image had appeared at a small size owing to the quality of the original from 1995. But for issue 32 of Spring and Summer 2014, I had a high resolution version redrawn. The Horses on the covers of 32, 33 and our 20th anniversary number, 34, had grown into a much more imposing part of the overall look and were reproduced at around two thirds of the height of the cover itself.

These variations were also matched by smaller changes in the inner layout. This is not the place to go into the minutiae of text typography (see my *The Printed Snow*, Happen*Stance* Press, 2015) but I have frequently experimented within standard conservative typographic variables with settings for the journal's contents. Using a relatively consistent design, issue 26 was set in Minion; issue 27, Bembo Book. Issue 28 returned to Minion, with a more spacious airy look than that in number 26, owing to increased leading. Issues 29 and 30 were again set in Bembo Book. Designed to replicate the 'ink squash' of the old metal type, it is a more robust version of the unsatisfactory Bembo I'd used for numbers 19 to 21. I set Issue 31 in Plantin, where its more rounded design gave a slightly 'softer' look to the text. For issues 32 to 35 I settled on the text face Clifford Pro, by the Japanese type designer Akira Koyabashi. A classic serif designed to function well in a digital environment, in keeping with historical serifs it has no bold weights. Its standard italic 'h' has too much of a curve in the final downstroke, taking it slightly too close to an italic 'b', for my taste. Fortunately, it has an alternate uncurved 'h' in the glyph palette with which I replace all occurrences of the standard italic 'h'. The gradual typographic improvement of the Horse's pages has marked my own increasing knowledge of this craft. That said, in a field marked by shocking amateurism, the Horse's layout was never dreadful.

It is difficult to single out highlights in these later issues' contents because to me, to a greater or lesser extent, they are all highlights. A glance at the covers (see pages 156 to 159) will give some idea of their scope. One of the pleasures of editing a journal which has reached a respected level is that accomplished writers are willing to write for the magazine. A little magazine can also be home for extended considerations you're unlikely to find elsewhere. Dennis O'Driscoll's overview of Kay Ryan's *The Best of It: New & Selected Poems*, which appeared in issue 28 (Spring 2012) was an example: over 6,000 words running to 17 pages in the journal. Unfortunately, though, one reference offended that remarkable poet. Some of her rhymes, O'Driscoll suggested, had the whiff of a rhyming dictionary. She wrote to me:

Naturally what I recall now is that he accused me—so wrongly!!—of resorting—ever!!—to the rhyming dictionary. I

have never cracked one; where would the fun be in that? [...]
I was horrified.

When Kay Ryan uses two sets of double exclamation points, you know she is annoyed.

Dennis, whom I had first met in 2008 (see my review memoir in Horse 33, Winter 2014/2015) was a remarkable combination: in person, hyper-gentlemanly; in critical prose, stringent. I casually mentioned in an email to him that I'd heard back from Kay about his review. I concluded, mischievously, 'but more on that another time'. Within minutes, he replied:

> I'm agog at your Kay Ryan news. Was the tone of her response a piqued one? I'm absolutely dying to know!

I emailed him back:

> I think the word that stood out was ...'horrified'. But *I* still love you Dennis!

By return came his response, typically gentlemanly:

> Now I feel horrified to have made Kay Ryan feel horrified....
> And I was under the illusion that I had written a balanced review that was immensely favourable on the whole.
>   Could I trouble you for her e-mail address please: I'd like to send her a calm and respectful note.

Little magazines are, at heart, sparkily human affairs. It is this human element, among other things, that makes them worth doing. Readers only see, of course, the formalised end product, as with published books, anthologies, etc. Poetry is an art of passionate engagement. It attracts individuals of like intensity.

* * *

Issue 29 ran a 'first book feature'—an invitation to ten poets to write about a first book by another poet which had been important to them, for whatever reason—personal, emotional, or because of its poetic technique. So, scattered throughout the issue were brief accounts by, for instance, Rory Waterman on R. S. Thomas, Wendy Cope on Douglas Dunn, Miriam Gamble on Derek Mahon, Ernest Hilbert on Frederick Seidel. As with much else in editing a journal, this idea had a root in my own experience. At the Aldeburgh Poetry Festival in November 2011 I had met for the first time the poet Oliver Reynolds. His debut collection, *Skevington's Daughter* (Faber, 1985) had had a profound effect on me when I was a literary loner, pre-Horse and even pre-*Spectrum*, in Ayrshire. I contributed in a small way my own account of a favourite first book in my editorial, which read in part:

> As we are young poets, so are we young readers of poetry. While we might not read with the critical acumen of our more mature selves, we read with energy hungry for self-develop-ment—love, if you will—and can be peremptory and absolute in our dismissals and enthusiasms. I was 26. The author of *Skevington's Daughter,* Oliver Reynolds, was 28. I found not only his subject matter fascinating but also the speaking voice behind the lines. That voice—ironic, witty, humane, histori-cally responsible, self-aware, sometimes anecdotal and seem-ing-confessional—sounded notably consistent throughout the book. Though occasionally Reynolds rhymed and scanned, generally he wrote in what appeared a relaxed free verse in which, as with [his opening narrative poem] 'Victoriana', the language was entirely in service to the narrative. He made it *look* easy. [...] Yet Reynolds clearly had the poet's relish for words: 'sesquipedalian', 'eidetic', 'lubricious', 'fluxive', 'coronal', 'beswick' and 'crenellation' all appeared, buffed up in lines of mingled register, but never seeming to draw too much at-tention to themselves. This young poet also had a fascination with recondite and unusual facts, sometimes relayed with throwaway irony—the 'Skevington's Daughter' of the book's title, for instance, was a medieval torture instrument.

The Special Feature—choosing a quirky or unexpected slant on something, and asking guest poets to respond—continued in issue 32, where I commissioned, in 'Poets' Lines', fourteen poets to write about one to six lines of poetry which had been especially significant for them. Though, as ever, it all depends on the quality of the responses, such features are fascinating for their insight into the human, anecdotal element of the art, with the general treatment being left to the individual writer. While I value literary criticism, many individuals of intelligence, engagement and insight can write illuminating criticism. Personal, anecdotal content can only be written out of memory and, sometimes, friendship; irreplaceable and unique, it is therefore at least as precious as an impersonal academic approach. For that reason, I have tried to encourage it frequently in the journal.

* * *

My chance attendance in late summer of 2013 at an event run in Edinburgh by Neu! Reekie! ('New Edinburgh'), a reading, animation and music series curated by Kevin Williamson and Michael Pedersen, led to the six remarkable poems by the Jamaican poet and novelist Kei Miller which kicked off issue 31. In the bar of the Edinburgh Film Theatre after his reading I asked if any of the poems had been published. 'None of them,' he said. I mentioned the ones I would be particularly interested in considering if he would send me them, which he did. They later formed part of his collection *The Cartographer Tries to Map A Way to Zion*, which won the Forward Prize for Best Collection in the autumn of 2014. I have scant respect for the expectation that one should kowtow to the whole ethos of such prizes. The whole tenor of the journal is against the easy inflation of hype, or seeing poetry as competition and its poets as racehorses for the titillation of a generally indifferent public. Yet the six poems we published from this book, like the book itself, opened up new spaces in their examination of, among other things, cultural appropriation via the making of maps. As with that of Amit Majmudar and Derek Walcott, such work brings exhilarating new subject matter to contemporary English-language poetry.

***

*Handing things on—the magazine and the younger poets—
contemporary critical culture—a lost scrupulousness*

Back in the early days of the magazine, Dana Gioia had written to me that what we were doing in it was not for ourselves; it was for the young. I disagreed at the time that the journal should be preparing the ground for what would come after us. I was, after all, almost a decade younger than Dana. I still felt I was one of 'the young'. I had no intention for the journal to become a sort of experimental seed ground for younger writers at the expense of quality. I wanted only to make each issue, as a finished object, the best thing it could be.

Fifteen or more years later, and this is something that began around issue 27 in 2011, it seems important to me that the magazine should have a sense of continuity. Accordingly I have supported, insofar as I've been able to without compromises, the work of younger writers such as Claire Askew, Niall Campbell, Richie McCaffery, Stewart Sanderson, Michael Pedersen and others—often Scottish-based, but not exclusively. This has also been the case in working with younger critics. The poetry culture needs its iconoclasts, its mavericks, its outsiders. Older writers who have been freed from the restrictions of eminence by neglect may naturally occupy that space by default. They are beyond the hope of sudden literary fame, with all that such hope implies of a canny—and, in the circumstances, perfectly sensible—positioning of one's self as unlikely to cause offence or 'speak truth to power'. It is a rare younger writer who is likely to stick his or her head above the parapet of the bland constructions of contemporary reviewing and criticism. Any young writer, unless they decide to model themself on a polemicist such as William Logan, has to negotiate a path in critical writing between the likelihood of causing offence and the duty to report honestly on their own impressions of the work they're writing about.

In part, the poetry world is to blame for the current state of affairs. Straightforwardness, which would have been considered commonplace forty or fifty years ago, would now be the subject of a backlash on social media. The community expectation in contemporary poetry is that almost everything is good. Therefore, relatively small cavils can be taken as large criticisms. Estimable critics, though, would traditionally have begun with the expectation that almost everything written at a particular time is either plain bad, or not of foremost quality. This should mean that the audience reading the reviewer would be less likely to expect praise. *The Dark Horse* prefers to encourage in its critical writing and reviewing a not-easily impressed, discerning, humanly-complex and all-rounded intelligent sensibility. Part of this means giving younger writers, as it were, permission to follow their instincts even for modest quibbles and the withholding of easy encomia. Almost all poetry written at any time is likely to last about as long as the magazine issue it appears in. (Any contemporary reader of, say, 50 year-old copies of *Poetry Review* or Tambimuttu's *Poetry London* can see how provisional and outdated most of those poems are now. Interestingly, prose seems to weather better: even reviews may have a *period* interest.)

The Horse attempts an aesthetic based upon a generous severity. Hopefully, this doesn't preclude humour or an awareness of the dazzling human variety, comedy and tragedy out of which the whole enterprise of poetry is born. Even so, it's a long way from Geoffrey Grigson, 'The Billhook', whose 1930s magazine *New Verse* was 'devoted', as Ian Hamilton wrote, 'to the joys of condemnation': 'We believe Mr R. H. as a poet to be absolutely a BORE,' it said of Rayner Heppenstall; Wallace Stevens' famous blackbird poem was 'an uneasy twinkle of sequins…forgetting the bird'; MacDiarmid's 'Second Hymn to Lenin' was 'seventy-seven pages of unvarying twitter'.

THE POETS' PROSE ISSUE
MUIR ON THE **BALLADS**
CANADIAN POETRY
FOR BEGINNERS **LARKIN**
& **MARRIAGE** THE SPIRIT
OF **EDWIN MORGAN**
SEAMUS HEANEY TALKS
POETRY IN SCOTLAND
WRITING THE POETIC
LIFE ◆ POEMS : WENDY
COPE ◆ ALASDAIR GRAY
MATTHEW SWEENEY &
AARON POOCHIGIAN

'Scotland's finest international literary journal. And, oddly
enough, one of the most consistently interesting journals
on American poetry.' —DANA GIOIA

26 | Winter / Spring 2011

Probably one of the most sophisticated covers typographically I've ever done for the Horse. This is Hypatia Sans, for a time one of my favourite sans serif typefaces, and Grafika—the Grafika to add a little flamboyance & visual pizzazz. I disliked the double 'R' of the Grafika in 'MARRIAGE', so replaced it—a typographical crime in some quarters—with the 'R' of Hypatia Sans, stretched and thinned to match, proportionately, the dimensions of its distinctive Art Deco companion. James Campbell reproduced this cover in his 'NB' column in the *TLS* of March 11, 2011, with a note about the design. He also quoted from Alasdair Gray's fine poem 'Old Moments', a memory of walking with his son: Alasdair's first appearance in the journal.

[155]

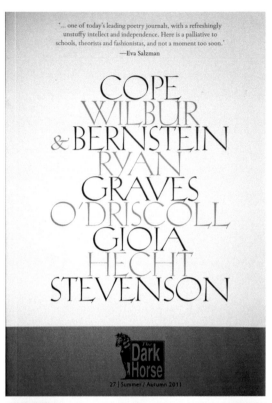

Both these covers show the influence of issue 26's bold typographic designs in trying to make the most of the beauty of particular typefaces. In the case of issue 27, above, this was Koch Antiqua, a sculpted face which has a handdrawn element. (It was also the titling face used on the cover of my collection *Notes for Lighting a Fire*.) The types used for issue 28 are Tacitus Pro Light and Expo Sans Light, both from the type designer Mark Jamra of Maine. The Horse logo had remained unchanged from that in issue 1; in these covers it was downsized and played only a modest part in the overall look, to give greater prominence to the bolder typography.

With issue 29 I dropped the magazine's logo in an attempt to have more possibilities for cover design; the main typeface is Stevens Titling, a useful and calligraphic variant to Trajan. Issue 30 was notable for the bold titling of the journal's name: it is Hypatia Sans Pro Extra Light, chosen because of the size at which it was being used. The serif for the definite article in the title is Caslon, for its 'Th' ligature. The lettering of the Contents is Soins Sans Pro.

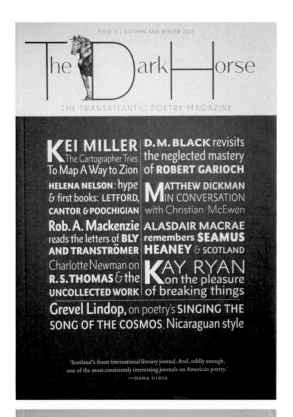

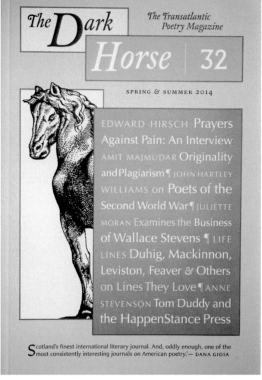

Like issue 26's, issue 31's, above, was another quite complex typographic cover—though it looks straightforward enough. Metro Nova in varying weights for the Contents' lettering, with Vanitas for the magazine's title and Landmark for the subtitle.

With issue 32, the Horse's image went full-size for the first time. The Contents' lettering was Optima, with Clifford Pro 18 for the magazine's title and Albertus for the issue number. The 'panel' motif was influenced, a touch, by literary magazine letterheads of the 1930s and 40s. The Dana Gioia quotation is set in Carter Sans.

Above: Issue 33 was published not long before Christmas 2014, so I thought it appropriate to give a seasonal feel to the colours on the cover. The Serifs are Clifford Pro (for the italic of the magazine title) and Albertina. Contents' lettering is Hypatia Sans, with the magazine's name in Hypatia Sans, with Sophia to add a touch of flamboyance. (Look at that ampersand!)

Below: A characteristically generous response to issue 29 from Dennis O'Driscoll in his typical, all capital, uncial style script.

The Horse goes to Edinburgh, London & New York—a celebration of 20 years

The Dark Horse celebrated its 20th anniversary with a special issue which, at 192 pages, was twice the extent of the usual number. Content-wise it was not only an honouring of contributors who had been significant in the history of the journal, but an introduction of new voices. For the first time ever, any indication of its contents, too, was dropped from the front cover. Instead, it presented a classical simplicity with the horses—two—featuring prominently and the magazine's title set in Eric Gill's Perpetua Titling. A full Contents list appeared on the back cover.

I felt the magazine's production values for this celebratory issue should be special. I had it printed on a beautiful, slightly off-white stock, Arcoprint Milk, 100gsm, in two colours— black and a classic red Pantone. The increased pagination made for a slightly stiffer spine, as I expected, though the Master bookbinder Tom McEwan of Ayrshire told me that the paper had been cut 'against the grain' by the printer, which would increase this effect. I joked that the anniversary number was more an object to sit on a mantelpiece and admire in its brick-like dimensions than to actually read.

This anniversary number upheld one of the journal's principles by printing three superb previously unpublished poems by the Scottish poet Ian Abbot, who had died in a car accident at the age of 42 in 1989, having published only a single book. How many of the younger writers in Scotland know anything of Ian Abbot? The poems were unearthed by the poet and critic Richie McCaffery, still in his twenties, during researches on Abbot in the National Library of Scotland.

In its entire history the Horse had never had a single launch event. So in June 2015 we had not one but *three* launches, in Edinburgh, London, and New York. I was helped to organise these by the young Edinburgh poet and cultural *animateur* Michael Pedersen. A well known performer on the Scottish 'spoken word' stage whose work can also bear scrutiny on the page, Michael played the enthusiastic and relentlessly optimistic pup to my lugubrious and droop-eyed bloodhound. He is at the time of writing a memorable figure with a bouffant hairdo which adds at least eighteen inches to his (already considerable) height. He had great experience in organising literary events; I had very little. We investigated several venues as possibles for the London launch. On the way to Vout-O-Reenees, 'The Crypt of the Roman Catholic Church of the English Martyrs', which we eventually chose, he said on the crowded subway carriage, 'Salena Godden really likes this venue.'

'Who's she?'

'A poet we had reading at Neu! Reekie!'

'I don't know her work.'

'She was excellent. I was showing a friend a video on YouTube of her performing one of her poems last night. It's called "The Good Cock".'

In the background noise of the subway, I misheard the poem's title.

'The *Woodcock*?' I said, suddenly animated. 'Does she have an interest in ornithology?'

'Eh, naw. Not the wood cock. The *good* cock. It's about finding a cock that—'

'I take it we're not talking barnyard fowl? Right, I get it.'

There was a pensive pause.

'What the fuck's a wood cock?' said Michael.

'Wading bird. *Scolopax rusticola*. Found in woods. I always fantasised as a teenager about finding its nest. Its eyes are set very high on the top of its head to look out for predators when probing the leaf litter for worms with its long beak. Famous for its habit of airlifting its chicks between its legs when disturbed to get them out of danger.'

'What the fuck's a wading bird?'

'A bird that usually feeds around estuaries and pond margins. Long legs. Long beak. The woodcock is highly unusual in being one of the few wading birds found among deciduous trees. It's exploited a unique niche.'

The natural world rarely features in Michael's poems.

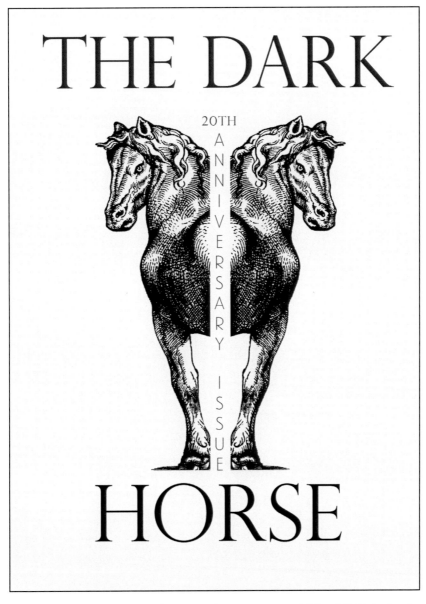

Front cover of the anniversary issue, number 34. Perpetua Titling MT Light for the magazine's name, with Landmark for the vertical text down the centre. I felt it was appropriate for this number to keep any other lettering off the cover. 192pp, printed early June 2015.

THE DARK HORSE

20TH ANNIVERSARY EDITION

Contents

£10.00 | $18.00

ISSN 1357-6720

For the first, and perhaps the last time, the issue Contents was added to the back cover with the anniversary number. Fifteen of the 55 contributors appeared in the issue for the first time.

* * *

Poets as editors—poetry politics—reciprocity between journals—the free space of the little magazine

Understandably enough, I have a special interest in poet-editors of little magazines and how they balance editing demands with their own writing. There have been, after all, famous ones: Jon Silkin of *Stand*, Ian Hamilton, Eliot with the *Criterion*; Geoffrey Grigson with *New Verse*, John Crowe Ransom in the US with the *Kenyon Review*. Editors are not, by definition, failed writers. I have always seen my own writing as central to everything else I do. I place great value upon that private discipline and practice, irrespective of the world's view and questions of public 'profile', which may have only an oblique connection with the quality of one's work. Without my own engagement in the art I could no more continue enterprises like *The Dark Horse* than a finch could fly with a single wing.

Surrounded by all the activity of other poets keen to have their work in the Horse, half-buried at times under a rising tide of such attempts at creativity, it's understandable that some poet-editors would find it difficult to keep faith with their own poetry and would ditch a journal so as to wholly focus on their own writing. After all, the latter is what most of one's potential contributors do.

When the manuscripts thud onto the doormat with relentless regularity; when the review copies pile up rapidly in their dozens and hundreds, accumulate in drifts of printed paper, teeter in metre-high towers; when they shout, silently, 'ego! ego!' and 'listen to me! in their unstoppable throngs, the final effect can be both dispiriting and devaluing. Looked at in one way, at least.

Looked at in another, all these attempts at utterance can be curiously cheering. At their most genuine they represent the human 'rage for order' in their attempt to create form and resist the drift toward oblivion and dissolution we all face, whether quickly or slowly—even when the attempt is dreadful, clichéd, or blithely ignorant of its own poverty of insight or technique.

Nor is editing necessarily damaging to one's own output. If you can crest the wave of exposure to all this submitted work, to arrive at what is good and what is bad in it, it can make you more discerning in your own poetry. Practically, too, managing a poetic life as an editor—I hesitate to say 'career' where poetry is concerned, unless one is using it as a verb as well as a noun—takes a judicious degree of balancing. You have to make sure the poet-identity is not subsumed by the editor-identity: that neither you nor the journal is compromised by poetry-politicking with the aim of using connections. It would be possible to do a good deal of that if you were so-minded. Not long after I began the magazine, I had a phone call in my caravan one May afternoon. It was another poet-editor. My first book, *The Shell House*, had recently been published. The editor said he—or she (I'm not saying)—had already sent it out for review. Very good, I said, a touch puzzled. There was a pause. Now, he was a reasonable, a nice, person, the voice at the other end of the line continued, but he was wondering when I would be sending out his own book for review in *my* magazine.

Taken aback by such a barefaced example of poetry politics and attempt to exert power, I said I would let him know, and put the phone down. I then sat and wrote my caller a letter and posted it that same afternoon, first class. In it I asked that he remove my book from review in his magazine until we had sorted out this business of reciprocity between editors. His book never was reviewed in the Horse. The editor in question, however, took the moral high ground, claiming that he had a '*duty*' to review significant new work in his magazine; what *I* decided to review in *my* magazine was my own business. Perhaps because I have regarded it as the flipside to my own writing, I have always found such compromises where the Horse is concerned practically impossible.

In the hall of my imagination, and in a variant on that dinner party game of ideal invited guests I would have all the past, remarkable contributors to *The Dark Horse* attend an enormous event—party—festival—in thanks for their contributions to this little magazine of which I remain proud. Like poetry itself, at heart a poetry magazine is a celebration of the human spirit beyond awards, issues of reputation and all the attendant palaver. It is a free space of expression that transcends commercialism and other involved interests. It aims for the high ranges even as it scrabbles in the foothills. I like to think that in the Horse this has been achieved with at least a skinkle of humour and a flash of that 'thread too bright for the eye' that my old friend and early encourager, George Mackay Brown, in quite another context, set down immortally in a poem long ago.

The poet A. B. Jackson is one of my oldest friends in poetry, whose work appeared in our inaugural issue and at various times since. I first met him in 1988 after hearing him read at the Courtyard Readings of the Scottish Poetry Library in its original premises in Tweeddale Court, Edinburgh. Here he becomes, to the best of my knowledge, the most northern reader ever of *The Dark Horse*. This photograph was taken at Ymerbukta, 78°18' N, 013°57' E—well within the Arctic Circle, near Spitzbergen, Svalbard, on 15 June 2015. Photograph by Ayo Yunyu Shih.

Readers from the Edinburgh 20th anniversary launch of *The Dark Horse*, held at the Voodoo Rooms on 4th June 2015: top, Claire Askew, whose first book, *This changes things*, apppeared from Bloodaxe in 2016; below, the legendary writer, artist and general polymath, Alasdair Gray. Photographs © Ryan McGoverne.

The two other main readers from the 20th Anniversary issue Edinburgh launch: top, Vicki Feaver, who was represented in the issue with four poems; and right, Douglas Dunn, a long-time contributor to the journal. Photographs © Ryan McGoverne.

The fiction writer Jennifer Goodrich, the magazine's US Assistant Editor, photographed in *The Dark Horse* office in Hastings-on-Hudson in June 2007. She is a native of the Bighorn Mountains of Wyoming and is married to the artist John Goodrich.

Marcia Menter, the US Contributing Editor, photographed in a café near the Fountain Pen Hospital in June 2016. See pages 123-4.

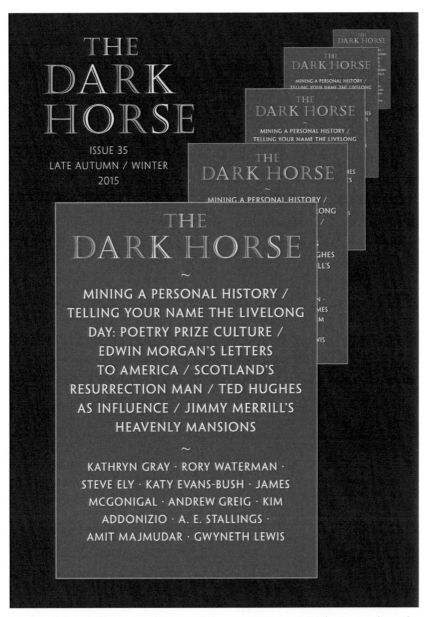

Issue 35 was the first in the history of the magazine to drop the Horse from the journal's cover. This let me use a dark ground colour—something not possible when using the Horse graphic. The issue included, among other highlights, Kathryn Gray's remarkable piece on the damage caused by poetry prize culture, as well as Steve Ely's piece examining crucial differences and similarities between his own upbringing and Ted Hughes'—an assimilated influence on his own work. I had met Steve at the inaugural Ted Hughes festival, held in Mexborough in Yorkshire in June 2015 and organised by Steve and Dominic Somers assisted by Ryan Madin; it focused on Hughes' often-overlooked childhood and adolescent years in the town. Ian Parks, another Mexborough poet, was also featured. Castellar for the magazine's title, with Penumbra Sans and Penumbra Half Serif for the other text and contributors' names.

The **DARK HORSE**

The
Transatlantic
Poetry
Magazine

LATE SPRING
&
SUMMER
2016

Andrew Sclater:
Meeting Stevie Smith

David Wheatley:
*Tweed, Minor Poets,
& G. S. Fraser*

Kathryn Maris & Alan Jenkins
In Conversation

Bethany W. Pope
*Herring and Blues:
Angus Martin & Kim Addonizio*

John Greening
Revisits Patricia Beer

⋆

Poems:
Chase Twichell Steve Ely
Rachael Boast Roisin Kelly
Louise Peterkin Marcia Menter

ISSUE 36

'... among the truly
outstanding poetry
magazines of the
English-speaking world.'

—Dennis O'Driscoll

A 'scoop' for this issue was Andrew Sclater's 21 page essay/review/memoir on Stevie Smith, whose *Collected Poems and Drawings* had just been published by Faber. Sclater first met Smith when at the age of 16 he invited her (she was then in her sixties) to his school to do a reading—leading to an unlikely and touching friendship. In the poetry, Chase Twichell, Rachael Boast, Roisin Kelly and Louise Peterkin appeared in the magazine for the first time, as did Kathryn Maris in prose.

This cover featured a redesigned Horse logo, produced by the graphic designer Marc Wilson, of the Scottish printer Philip Wilson's firm, Love and Humphries. A new, more streamlined Horse, ready for the magazine's canter into its third decade.

A NOTE ON THE TYPES

The text of *The Dark Horse: The Making of a Little Magazine*
is set primarily in Miller, designed by Matthew Carter
and released in 1997. It is a 'Scotch Roman',
a category of type for historical reasons very popular in America,
and follows the original style in having both roman
and italic small capitals. The style was developed from types
cut by Richard Austin between 1810 and 1820
at the Edinburgh type foundries
of Alexander Wilson and William Miller.

Captions and Index are set in Matthew Carter's rugged, slightly
sculptural sans serif Carter Sans, which makes
a useful companion face for the plain gravitas of Miller.